PENNY KITTLE

MW01133809

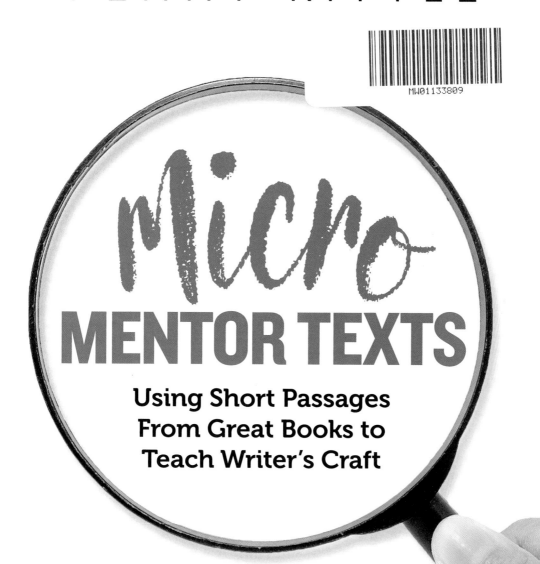

Micro
MENTOR TEXTS

Using Short Passages From Great Books to Teach Writer's Craft

For Maisie and Lila... *may you find words that delight and surprise you...*
in books, of course, but also in your stories and ideas that will tumble
inside of you and grow as you write them.

Senior Vice President and Publisher: Tara Welty
Acquisitions Editor: Lois Bridges
Editorial Director: Sarah Longhi
Development Editor: Raymond Coutu
Senior Editor: Shelley Griffin
Production Editor: Danny Miller
Creative Director: Tannaz Fassihi
Interior Designer: Maria Lilja

Scholastic is not responsible for the content of third-party websites and does not endorse any site or imply that the information on the site is error-free, correct, accurate, or reliable.

Photos ©: cover: Scholastic Inc.; cover, 1, 31: Shutterstock.com. All other photos by Jessica Scranton © Scholastic Inc.

Excerpts from: *Alice Austen Lived Here* © 2022 by Alex Gino. Used by permission of Scholastic Inc.; *Alone* © 2021 by Megan E. Freeman. Used by permission of Simon & Schuster Children's Publishing Division, a division of Simon & Schuster, Inc.; *Amelia and Eleanor Go For a Ride* © 1999 by Pam Muñoz Ryan. Used by permission of Scholastic Inc.; *Caged Warrior* © 2014 by Alan Lawrence Sitomer. Used by permission of Hachette Book Group, Inc. and Writers House; *Caprice* © 2022 by Coe Booth. Used by permission of Scholastic Inc.; *Countdown* © 2010 by Deborah Wiles. Used by permission of Scholastic Inc.; *Dear Mrs. LaRue* © 2002 by Mark Teague. Used by permission of Scholastic Inc.; *The Dreamer* © 2010 by Pam Muñoz Ryan. Used by permission of Scholastic Inc.; *Duke Ellington* © 1998 by Andrea Davis Pinkney. Used by permission of Hachette Book Group, Inc.; *Falling Down the Page* © 2009 by Georgia Heard. Originally published by Roaring Brook Press. Used by permission of Curtis Brown, Ltd.; *Fire Becomes Her* © 2022 by Rosiee Thor. Used by permission of Scholastic Inc.; *The Great Gracie Chase: Stop That Dog!* © 2001 by Cynthia Rylant. Used by permission of Scholastic Inc.; *The Great Greene Heist* © 2014 by Varian Johnson. Used by permission of Scholastic Inc.; *Harry Potter and the Sorcerer's Stone* © 1997 by J. K. Rowling. Published by Scholastic Inc.; *Hurricane Child* © 2018 by Kacen Callender. Used by permission of Scholastic Inc.; *If I Ever Get Out of Here* © 2013 by Eric Gansworth. Used by permission of Scholastic Inc.; *Illegal* © 2020 by Francisco X. Stork. Used by permission of Scholastic Inc.; *Infinity Ring: Curse of the Ancients* © 2013 by Matt de la Peña. Used by permission of Scholastic Inc.; *It's the End of the World and I'm in My Bathing Suit* © 2022 by Justin A. Reynolds. Used by permission of Scholastic Inc.; *King and the Dragonflies* © 2020 by Kacen Callender. Used by permission of Scholastic Inc.; *Land of the Cranes* © 2020 by Aida Salazar. Used by permission of Scholastic Inc.; *The Light in Hidden Places* © 2020 by Sharon Cameron. Used by permission of Scholastic Inc.; *Lines of Courage* © 2022 by Jennifer A. Nielsen. Used by permission of Scholastic Inc.; *The Lines We Cross* © 2017 by Randa Abdel-Fattah. Used by permission of Scholastic Inc.; *The Living* © 2013 by Matt de la Peña. Used by permission of Random House Children's Books, a division of Penguin Random House LLC, and Writers House LLC; *Martin Rising* © 2018 by Andrea Davis Pinkney. Used by permission of Scholastic Inc.; *Me, Frida, and the Secret of the Peacock Ring* © 2018 by Angela Cervantes. Used by permission of Scholastic Inc.; *The Moon Within* © 2019 by Aida Salazar. Used by permission of Scholastic Inc.; *Of Mice and Men* © 1937 by John Steinbeck. Used by permission of Penguin Young Readers Group, a division of Penguin Random House LLC; *The Paper Boy* © 1996 by Dav Pilkey. Used by permission of Scholastic Inc.; *The Race of the Century* © 2022 by Neal Bascomb. Used by permission of Scholastic Inc.; *The Red Pencil* © 2014 by Andrea Davis Pinkney. Used by permission of Hachette Book Group, Inc.; *Refugee* © 2017 by Alan Gratz. Used by permission of Scholastic Inc.; "Return Policy", Imelda's Shoes, Portland, Oregon used by permission of Pamela B. Coven; *Rhythm Ride* © 2015 by Andrea Davis Pinkney. Used by permission of Roaring Brook Press, a division of Holtzbrinck Publishing Holdings Limited Partnership; *Rick* © 2020 by Alex Gino. Used by permission of Scholastic Inc.; *Shadowshaper* © 2015 by Daniel José Older. Used by permission of Scholastic Inc.; *The Sky Is Everywhere* © 2010 by Jandy Nelson. Used by permission of Penguin Young Readers Group, a division of Penguin Random House LLC, and Pippin Properties, Inc.; *Somewhere in the Darkness* © 1992 by Walter Dean Myers. Used by permission of Scholastic Inc.; *Sunrise Over Fallujah* © 2008 by Walter Dean Meyers. Used by permission of Scholastic Inc.; *Vacancy* © 2021 by K. R. Alexander. Used by permission of Scholastic Inc.; *Watercress* © 2021 by Andrea Wang. Used by permission of Holiday House Publishing, Inc.; *When Marian Sang* © 2002 by Pam Muñoz Ryan. Used by permission of Scholastic Inc.; *Where the Crawdads Sing* © 2018 by Delia Owens. Used by permission of Penguin Young Readers Group, a division of Penguin Random House LLC; *A Wish in the Dark* © 2020 by Christina Soontornvat. Used by permission of Candlewick Press; *With the Might of Angels* © 2011 by Andrea Davis Pinkney. Used by permission of Scholastic Inc.; *Zac & Mia* © 2014 by A. J. Betts. Used by permission of HarperCollins Children's Books, a division of HarperCollins Publishers. All rights reserved.

No part of this publication may be reproduced in whole or in part, or stored in a retrieval system, or transmitted in any form or by any means, electronic, mechanical, photocopying, recording, or otherwise, without written permission of the publisher. For information regarding permission, write to Scholastic Inc., 557 Broadway, New York, NY 10012. Copyright © 2022 by Penny Kittle. All rights reserved. Published by Scholastic Inc. Printed in the U.S.A. ISBN 978-1-338-78907-2 • SCHOLASTIC and associated logos are trademarks and/or registered trademarks of Scholastic Inc. Other company names, brand names, and product names are the property and/or respective owners. Scholastic does not endorse any product or business entity mentioned herein.

1 2 3 4 5 6 7 8 9 10   40   31 30 29 28 27 26 25 24 23 22

Scholastic Inc., 557 Broadway, New York, NY 10012

Contents

Go to scholastic.com/MicroMentorResources to find videos and other resources!

Featured Authors and Books

Foreword

I grew up believing there was a massive difference between writing for school and writing for *real*. In middle school and most of high school, to me, writing meant five-paragraph essays and scripted reading logs and blue-book proof that I could identify the themes and symbolism in each of the ancient novels assigned to the whole class. Even the occasional creative writing unit verged on algebra. "First we get our characters up in a tree," I remember one teacher explaining, while projecting a story graph. "Then we throw rocks at them, and then we get them down. Follow this formula, class, and you'll do fine. Are we ready?" My classmates and I sat there, staring at the graph, paralyzed. And when I finally got going, writing a story felt about as natural as playing basketball in a suit of armor.

But when it came to creative writing, I was living a double life. Sure, I dragged my feet in class, but each night before bed I would lay on my stomach, on my bedroom floor, and sketch spoken-word-style poems into secret notebooks. "Writing for real" meant writing without rules. It meant writing about my life, my broken heart, and all the things that confused me. I cherished those poems so much, I'd revise them over and over, each stanza, each line, each word. And when a poem finally felt right, I would carefully write by hand a final draft into a special black journal, one I kept hidden in a shoebox beneath my bed.

But things changed when I entered eleventh grade and was assigned a different kind of teacher. Miss Blizzard. For our first whole-class read, she passed out copies of *The House on Mango Street* by Sandra Cisneros. I was shocked to discover a protagonist who was Mexican like me. That lived in a community like mine. That narrated in a voice reminiscent of the way my friends and I talked around the neighborhood. Then, at the end of the year, instead of handing me the final, Miss Blizzard handed me 12 blank sheets of paper and whispered in my ear, "I gave you an A on the test. All I want you to do is write whatever comes to mind for the next two hours." I was beyond confused. But, hey, I got an A, so I started working. And for the first time in my life, I found myself writing at school the way I wrote at home. I didn't look up until the bell rang.

When we were all filing out of the classroom that day, Miss Blizzard stopped me and asked, "Do you know why I did that?" I shook my head. "Because you're a really interesting writer, Matt. And I couldn't wait to see what you'd come up with if you had two straight hours to write."

Miss Blizzard didn't help much with the five-paragraph essay.

But she sure did change my life.

Penny Kittle's brilliant book, *Micro Mentor Texts*, is an invitation for teachers to forever change the way their students engage with writing in the classroom. Truth is, the best writing teacher in the world is great literature. But in this book, Penny not only curates a wonderful range of diverse short passages, she also invites teachers and students to look closely at the craft moves writers have made before sharing some of her own rich insights about each passage. She then invites students to imitate some of the craft moves they've just observed, while writing from whatever space feels most exciting to them. But what I find truly invaluable about this book is the modeling Penny does before she invites students to write.

There's so much mystery around great writing. Young people often believe favorite books fall out of the sky, or that they're the work of genius. In truth, most great books are written by ordinary people who are willing to work hard. Penny shows great vulnerability by inviting readers into her own process as she writes alongside published works. She speaks "aloud" as she composes lines, crosses out words, deletes entire paragraphs, rejoices over some new discovery. In essence, she's modeling the writer's process so that her readers will feel emboldened to model the process in their own classrooms. Over the years, I've done a lot of visiting writer's workshops, and the most successful of them all have one thing in common: The teacher is brave enough to write alongside her students. Penny's book helps to demystify the writing process. Writing is something we all can do. It's something we can all get better at.

Penny's book also helps to demystify the *teaching* of writing. All educators can inspire students to "write for real" inside their classrooms, the way Miss Blizzard inspired me. And this book is a wonderful place to start.

—**MATT DE LA PEÑA,** *New York Times* bestselling author
and Newbery Medal winner for *Last Stop on Market Street*

"The story of what goes on in readers is what we need most as writers, not evaluation of the quality of our writing or advice about how to fix it but an accurate account of what our words did to readers. We need to learn to feel those readers on the other end of our line. When are they with us? When are their minds wandering? What are they thinking and feeling? What do they hear us saying?"

—Peter Elbow

Introduction

2014. That is the year I imagined this book. I wrote an essay about my love of reading for *Open a World of Possible* at the request of my first editor, Lois Bridges. When it was published, I was excited to learn how a love of reading began and remained in the hearts and minds of so many authors and educators I admired. Lois and I met in a crammed hallway at the NCTE annual conference that fall, and I told her we must also open a world of possible in *writing*. That is my purpose for writing this book.

Evidence of writer's craft can be found in the books that are already in our classrooms, and we can teach the possibilities of that craft. We can ignite curiosity and joy in writing as we explore with our students gorgeous passages in novels, picture books, poetry, and nonfiction, and practice the moves their authors make.

We know that students who practice writing become stronger writers, even on tests. However, writing for tests snuffs out joy. Students who practice test-taking too much leave schools uninterested in writing and without the confidence to do anything beyond summarize and explain. I know because those students fill my college classroom each fall.

The Importance of Centering Students: A Bit of History

To explain how that happened, you have to understand a collision of forces from 40 years ago. The '80s were known for shoulder pads and short shorts, music videos and mustaches, pajama pants and poofy hair. (I know. The evidence is in my photo albums.) The decade was wacky, so maybe that's why politicians were suddenly very concerned about what was happening in schools. In 1983, *A Nation at Risk: The Imperative for Educational Reform*, published by the United States National Commission on Excellence in Education, claimed schools suffered from uneven standards, which left students ill-prepared for the future. It warned, "If an unfriendly foreign power had attempted to impose on America the mediocre educational performance that exists today, we might well have viewed it as an act of war." I was teaching 34 sweet third graders in the desert in California when I read the report. I couldn't reconcile the politics of fear with the commitment and goodwill I saw in my colleagues. A central recommendation of the report was the adoption of rigorous standards, along with state and national tests to measure achievement.

A TURNING POINT IN WRITING INSTRUCTION

That same year, Donald H. Graves published *Writing: Teachers and Children at Work*, a culmination of his 1978 Ford Foundation study "Balance the Basics: Let Them Write" and his daily observation in classrooms at Atkinson Elementary School. The book presented a radical vision for what young writers could do. Graves believed we could raise imaginative, original thinkers. His research positioned writing as central to reading development. After all, young writers read their own stories again and again, strengthening their word recognition and understanding of grammar—of how language "works." As Thomas Newkirk noted, "Graves established an undeniable fact—children could take on the role of writers, and classrooms could be organized to support this writing" (2013). This book started a worldwide movement that placed individualized, differentiated instruction at the center of the teaching of writing. A colleague down the hall handed me a copy in my second year of teaching, and it has influenced my work ever since.

Graves' colleague, Donald M. Murray, had been writing about similar ideas and practicing them with first-year students at the University of New Hampshire for decades. In fact, the two Dons had offices just down the hall from each other in Hamilton-Smith Hall. Murray spoke of teaching his college students the moves that writers make. He suggested that if students were to progress, first they must *cease to imagine themselves as students* and instead take on the *identity of writers*. Why? The writing instruction Murray observed in high schools was tightly regulated: "Topics were assigned; all errors were marked; outlines required for all longer papers; a structure (five paragraphs) imposed; all papers graded; no readers other than the teacher" (2013). Sounds familiar, doesn't it? These practices still govern writing instruction for thousands of students today.

Rigidity and formula belie the reason any of us write. We write because we have something to say that matters to us. Writers know their intended audience, choose their own subjects, play with structure, and choose a form and voice that are appropriate for the audience. Schools have been seduced by uniformity, which makes sense if your goal is to raise strong test-takers, but not if you're trying to raise flexible, empowered writers.

As Tom Newkirk wrote, "How radical to imagine that ideas like rehearsal, or drafting, or publication would be relevant to six-year-olds. What a leap of imagination he took to think that 'the writing process' was important for children struggling to break the code of literacy" (2013). Graves named what that idea means for teachers:

> "Many similarities were seen in the children when they wrote, but as the study progressed, *individual exceptions* to the data increased in dominance. *In short, every child had behavioral characteristics in the writing process that applied to that child alone*. It is our contention, based on this information, that such variability *demands* a waiting, responsive type of teaching" (Graves, 1980; italics mine).

THE ROLE OF THE RESPONSIVE TEACHER

Responsive teachers provide vision, modeling, and support based on the needs of individual students. They *lead* writers instead of simply assigning tasks and evaluating them. You can see how that approach conflicts with the expectation that all students perform on the same tests in the same way. That might work for physics or algebra, but for writing? No.

In 1983, policy makers studied *test scores*. Murray and Graves (and soon after Atwell, Hansen, Newkirk, Romano, Rief, and legions of practicing teachers) studied *students*. Teacher-researchers studied the process of how students learn to write well and the classroom conditions that made that learning more likely. My entire career has been spent firmly in that camp: I want to help raise writers with voice and vision.

Why This Book Now?

Forty years after "A Nation at Risk," the standardization of curriculum—rigidity and formula—continues to be more common than not, and many young writers bear its scars. It is likely you do as well. The holistic view of supporting and encouraging young writers is often swamped by a sea of tests and standards.

But there is hope.

Your students can and will learn that a book is a treasure chest of craft moves—the moves that skilled writers use. They can and will begin to name those moves and use them themselves. They will learn a wide range of writing skills from grammar in context, varied sentence structure—both the art and the feel for cohesion and style—as well as all the ways a writer is an artist of words. Students will learn how to:

- Reveal a setting and characters using sensory details.
- Compose powerful sentences and paragraphs.
- Capture conversations between and within characters.
- Use scenes as building blocks in longer narratives.
- Craft voice in fiction, poetry, biography, and narrative nonfiction.
- Use literary devices effectively.
- Combine craft moves across texts.

This is exciting, liberating work. You and your students will begin to see writer's craft everywhere. You will become explorers, collectors, and experimenters.

Teaching With Mentor Texts

Whether you're experienced working with mentor texts or not, this book is for you.

IF YOU'RE NEW TO WORKING WITH MENTOR TEXTS...

Start small. Begin with one craft move. Study one of the passages in this book, write your own passage inspired by it, and then show students what you've done. Invite them to do the same. Begin collecting passages that demonstrate your chosen craft move. Celebrate students who find evidence of the move in the books they are reading. You will open a window into how reading and writing are intimately connected, both in teaching and in learning. The study of craft moves enriches both. You'll create a bridge between books and your young writers.

IF YOU'RE ALREADY COMFORTABLE WORKING WITH MENTOR TEXTS...

This book will help you imagine a new way to work with them. So much can be taught and learned from studying a small passage together. Short passages make it easy to connect craft moves across texts. We can target our instruction on individual craft moves and reinforce that understanding throughout the school year and across genres. *Micro Mentor Texts* will be a bridge between the teaching of writing and the rich and varied reading lives of your students. Micro mentor texts are everywhere! As students collect passages and share them, they learn new ways to imagine these craft moves in their own writing.

Writers will learn how to lift life's everyday moments into the minds of readers. Reading and writing are and have always been united. When we intentionally connect them in our teaching, we strengthen students' abilities in both. I wrote *Micro Mentor Texts* to show you how I make that connection.

How I Chose the Micro Mentor Texts in This Book

Choosing texts for this book was a joy. I read stacks of picture books, chapter books, and YA novels, written by authors I've known for decades, as well as many that are new to me. I intentionally selected authors and characters from a range of cultural backgrounds. Genres include fiction, poetry, biography, and narrative nonfiction. And since this book's publication, so many more wonderful books for young people have been released! Every day I read them with wonder. There are so many original and thoughtful ways to tell a story or explain a moment in history. And I'm always highlighting passages for possible use in my teaching. I hope this book inspires you to do the same. Here's to the authors who fill our lives with such beauty.

A Close-Up Look at a Craft Lesson

Thirty-eight years of teaching in K-college classrooms have shown me the magic of micro mentor texts. This book will empower you to teach big ideas in writing from small texts. It is a practice that will never stop giving. Your classroom library is full of passages right now that you can study with students.

WHAT EACH CHAPTER CONTAINS

In each chapter, you will find a list of what I notice in one passage from a great book— or one micro mentor text.

King and the Dragonflies by Kacen Callender	Details I Notice
I like to look for my brother in the afternoon by the bayou, on the long and hot and [...] m school, [...] ad that [...] thorny [...] fluffy [...] he trees [...] vines, [...] noise [...] heir tunes. [...] eem to [...] ey've got [...] only I'd [...] d wait	• "...the long and hot and sweaty walk..." could have been punctuated as "long, hot, and sweaty," but the repeating conjunction (and) makes the walk *feel longer* and drawn out. The punctuation makes me trudge through this sentence. • Callender's description is a 58-word sentence. It tires me to read it! I'm sure that was intentional. • "The road weaves" is personification: as if the road is a living thing. This literary device is repeated when the author says the trees "seem to be watching, like they have a secret to tell me." The world is alive around our character, almost like the setting is a character as well. • The sensory details include both sight and sound. Notice the impact of sound on your understanding. You might not recognize the sound of cicadas if you are from the north, but all readers likely know the sound of birds.

1a Reveal Setting With Sensory Details

FIRST: NOTICE

In the following chart, in the first column, is a short passage that reveals a setting from a book that you may already have in your classroom library: *King and the Dragonflies* by Kacen Callender, which won the 2021 National Book Award for Young People's Literature.

What do you notice in the passage? Try to name a few craft moves *before you read* "Details I Notice" in the column I've filled in on the right. It's tempting to just jump to my observations, isn't it? But this practice we are doing is not about finding answer; it is about practicing close attention to the moves writers make.

So, try it... don't even glance at that column on the right. What do you notice?

Then you'll practice noticing and applying craft moves with me, as I draft a passage of my own.

SECOND: IMITATE

Try the move with me. Choose a place that is familiar. Perhaps think aloud as you list possibilities: the soccer field, the cafeteria, your classroom, the town library, a favorite restaurant, a room in your house.

I choose my neighborhood.

I speak as I model for students: "Callender begins this scene with the feel of a long walk, so I will try that using the first phrase they[2] did: 'I like to....'"

> I like to follow my dog on a long walk in our neighborhood. I kick acorns off the driveway as we begin and Julius charges after them, barking as the acorns bounce and scatter into the lawn.

YOUR TURN

On the next page are four short passages from beautiful pieces of literature that I have used with students. Each one reveals a setting to readers. As I did in the chart in the previous section with the passage from *King and the Dragonflies*, you will write what you notice about the writer's craft. This practice fine-tunes your skills in noticing and naming moves and prepares you w̶

Me, Frida, and the Secret of the Peacock Ring by Angela Cervantes

Paloma lifted her suitcase onto the bed in her new room, which was painted a bright, cheerful yellow. She felt like a sunflower had swallowed her up, and she liked it. In Kansas, her walls were "barely beige." Paloma's mom had called it a "nice neutral color" that would match everything, but Paloma argued that "barely beige" was a crayon box reject and an insult to flowers and rainbows. At home, she covered the barely beige walls with as many posters as she could.

Sunrise Over Fallujah by Walter Dean Myers

The afternoon sky was dazzling white above the small village. The room we entered was dark and smelly and for a moment I was blinded by the contrast. There were only a few candles lit against one wall. When my eyes became accustomed to the darkness I saw that there were mats lined up along the floor. There were a few women on them, but most of the bodies lying side by side were children.

From there, I give you a collection of micro mentor texts to use with your students. You will later write details you notice about them (as I did in the "Imitate" section) and then model the problem-solving that powers imitation. In the process, you will learn the twin powers of writing with students: to bind a classroom community and to share the joy of crafting sentences.

Their Turn: Independent Practice

Independent practice is an essential move that anchors the learning of a craft move. Guided practice in noticing details and in using them to enliven writing is important, but we want students to gather their own collections of micro mentor texts. Sometimes we underestimate what students can do. A student may find weak examples (in your mind) of sensory details... a yellow dress, a wilted flower, for example. But if that student has never thought about elements of writer's craft before, this is an important first step. I think of independent practice on a continuum. First simple examples; soon more layered, complex, vivid ones.

Last, I offer ideas for leading your students to collect their own micro mentor texts independently—and use them to inspire their own writing.

Imagine your favorite library. In mine, books fill shelves that reach so high you need a moving ladder to navigate them. There are balconies and windows and strings of twinkling lights. There are thousands of books.

Now flip that image to rows of empty shelves. The books are missing because people never had the courage to write them. They lost their passion for writing while swimming in a sea of rules and test prep. Imagine the stories and voices we will never hear because we were too busy hustling to standardize kids. It's like wandering in an art gallery of empty frames. Let's reimagine the teaching of writing and empower students to write their lives.

Chapter 1

Igniting the Imagination With Sensory Details

"I wasn't aware that words could hold so much. I didn't know a sentence could be so full."

—Delia Owens, *Where the Crawdads Sing*

Today it seems that we're all shouting to be heard in this busy world. The quiet comes between a reader and a text, one voice at a time. When we read, we want each word to matter. How do texts get our complete attention? By activating our senses through exquisite craft. A text composed with symmetry and music demands a closer look. When a writer brings us close to the smoky smell of an outdoor fire, we engage. The voice of a text rises and calls to us: *Pay attention. I have something to tell just to* you.

Specific, clear, original details—we simply wouldn't be readers without them. They connect experiences of a reader to a character's actions and understandings. We read *the sun twinkled across the water* and enter a setting that is as individual as a reader imagines it to be. It is built on that reader's experience with the sun, with water, and with other sensations that aren't mentioned, but are felt by the reader—the breeze against bare skin, the growl of hunger in the belly. The image itself grows larger than the text in the mind of an engaged reader.

The right details at just the right moment help readers co-create an imagined world with an author. The magic in reading is being transported across time, across place—from where we are to another world where this story unfolds. Details are at the heart of storytelling, certainly, and creating them is a craft move that is used in writing every kind of text.

We know a good story is a balance of showing *and* telling. Too many details, and a story crawls from one page to the next. Our minds wander. And too few? Well, we find ourselves half-listening; we aren't entering the story, we're just hearing it told. A close study of how authors maneuver that balance strengthens students' analytical skills as it deepens their enjoyment of both reading and writing.

Readers want to know where they are when they enter a story. Details tell them. They help them create a mental image as they read, which is essential to comprehension. Often the opening scene reveals a character moving in a place. That place—the setting—becomes a central part of the story. The author shows us when in history the story takes place. We feel the weather. We piece together the streets that make up a town, or the trails followed home from school, and we develop a feeling for the setting as characters move through it.

Here is a glimpse of a setting revealed in just four sentences:

> *Very few people in the whole world had ever flown at night, and Amelia was one of them. Amelia's eyes sparkled, "The stars glitter all about and seem close enough to touch. At higher elevations, the clouds below shine white with dark islands where the night sea shows through. I've seen the planet Venus setting on the horizon, and I've circled cities of twinkling lights."*
> —Pam Muñoz Ryan, *Amelia and Eleanor Go for a Ride*

Ryan's language *transports* us to a peaceful night sky. We are inside the plane beside Amelia Earhart and her passenger, Eleanor Roosevelt, on a daring flight in 1933. I draw on my experiences looking up at the stars to imagine the glitter they saw. Then I imagine looking down through the clouds to a dark sea. I can't picture what Venus looks like, so I imagine it. Other readers who have spent time with a telescope might instantly recall the size and shape of Venus and see more precise details as they read the same passage. We bring our experiences and our imaginations to our reading.

The layers of writer's craft are evident in those few sentences. You may have noticed the repeated "s" sounds throughout or heard the alliteration (repeated initial consonant sounds in *circled cities*) and consonance (recurrence of "t" in proximity: *twinkling lights*). These are powerful when read aloud to students. Authors labor over sentences, so let's pay close attention to them.[1] The more we teach students to notice writer's craft, the more likely they will begin to use craft moves in their own writing.

---

[1] Matt de la Peña once told me he can spend 90 minutes on one sentence, studying it, shaping it, and listening to it until it feels right to him.

1a Reveal Setting With Sensory Details

FIRST: NOTICE

In the following chart, in the first column, is a short passage that reveals a setting from a book that you may already have in your classroom library: *King and the Dragonflies* by Kacen Callender, which won the 2021 National Book Award for Young People's Literature.

What do you notice in the passage? Try to name a few craft moves *before you read* "Details I Notice" in the column I've filled in on the right. It's tempting to just jump to my observations, isn't it? But this practice we are doing is not about finding answers; it is about practicing close attention to the moves writers make.

So, try it… don't even glance at that column on the right. What do you notice?

King and the Dragonflies by Kacen Callender	Details I Notice
I like to look for my brother in the afternoon by the bayou, on the long and hot and sweaty walk back from school, down the hard dirt road that weaves between the thorny bushes with their big fluffy leaves, and through the trees with their moss and vines, cicadas making their noise and birds whistling their tunes. Those trees always seem to be watching. Like they've got a secret to tell me, if only I'd stop for a second and wait and listen.	• "…the long and hot and sweaty walk…" could have been punctuated as "long, hot, and sweaty," but the repeating conjunction (and) makes the walk *feel longer* and drawn out. The punctuation makes me trudge through this sentence. • Callender's description is a 58-word sentence. It tires me to read it! I'm sure that was intentional. • "The road weaves" is personification: as if the road is a living thing. This literary *device* is repeated when the author says the trees "seem to be watching, like they have a secret to tell me." The world is alive around our character, almost like the setting is a character as well. • The sensory details include both sight and sound. Notice the impact of sound on your understanding. You might not recognize the sound of cicadas if you are from the north, but all readers likely know the sound of birds.

SECOND: IMITATE

Try the move with me. Choose a place that is familiar. Perhaps think aloud as you list possibilities: the soccer field, the cafeteria, your classroom, the town library, a favorite restaurant, a room in your house.

I choose my neighborhood.

I speak as I model for students: "Callender begins this scene with the feel of a long walk, so I will try that using the first phrase they[2] did: 'I like to....'"

> *I like to follow my dog on a long walk in our neighborhood. I kick acorns off the driveway as we begin and Julius charges after them, barking as the acorns bounce and scatter into the lawn.*

I continue speaking, "I look back at Callender's passage and notice that the road weaves *between* things and Callender names sounds they hear as they walk, so I will try both of those moves to create details about my road."

> *We walk down the street between the deep quiet of vacation homes and the shadows cast by tall trees heavy with leaves. I hear my neighbor's dog yipping through the screen door...I hear...*

Students needn't imitate Callender's passage so closely. They might use one or both craft moves I tried above.[3] I continue to speak, going back to the passage for inspiration as I work ("Look at their verbs!" I might say). Once I have demonstrated for a minute or two, I invite students to try what I've demonstrated in their own notebooks.

Instead of having all students write about the same setting, I encourage each of them to choose a place they know well because they will be more successful if they can see the setting clearly and want to write about it, and I avoid the inherent competition that happens when students all write about the same thing.[4]

---

[2] Kacen Callender is nonbinary and uses the pronouns "they/them."

[3] I try to maintain a balance between imitation and creation. Thus, students might focus on sound as they write, spending several minutes just listing the sounds they hear. They might also try an imitation of two descriptive phrases separated by *between*.

[4] "We seek diversity, not proficient mediocrity." –Donald M. Murray

I continue working on my model for a minute or two to settle students into working independently.[5] I've found that when I do this, students are less likely to ask for my help. They see themselves as I see them: as writers who can solve their own writing problems and call upon me when help is truly needed.

After five minutes or so of practice, I have students share their passages (or just their thinking) in pairs. As students share, I wander among them and listen. You will likely be excited by their experiments, and I encourage you to bring your class together and invite some students to share what they have written. The students will be treated to a variety of settings and possibilities. I celebrate the close attention to detail that causes settings to become vivid in our minds.

My students and I create an anchor chart together to capture the thinking that helps make a setting clear. Doing that cements this new practice as students get back to work on their reading and their writing.

 TIP

When Possible, Share the Whole Book

Whenever I use a passage from a book during a writing lesson, I show students the book it came from. Students who are curious about the passage I've chosen or intrigued by the writer's craft will perhaps want to read the whole book. Score!

YOUR TURN

What follows are four short passages from beautiful pieces of literature that I have used with students. Each one reveals a setting to readers. As I did in the chart in the previous section with the passage from *King and the Dragonflies*, you will write what you notice about the writer's craft. This practice fine-tunes your skills in noticing and naming moves and prepares you well for your next lessons.[6]

---

[5] Don Graves found in his research that students paid more attention to their writing when the teacher was also writing.

[6] Don't rely too heavily on my lessons. You are going to learn more from your own observations and the noticings of your wise students.

Select a passage that you feel is a good fit for your students and use it to demonstrate writing with them. Be sure to speak as you compose in front of students.[7]

Land of the Cranes by Aida Salazar

I know my school's shiny floors
a broken water fountain
and boxed chocolate milk
I buy for fifty cents.

I know Ms. Martinez
        and her
happy handshakes
        at her door
before each fourth grade morning.

Land of the Cranes by Aida Salazar

But right now our happiness is big and wide
because she looks like Belle dancing a waltz
with gruff Tio Juan in her *Beauty and the Beast*
backyard ballroom.

Paper flowers all around the tall, rented canopy
yellow ribbons woven in the chain-link fence.

Me, Frida, and the Secret of the Peacock Ring by Angela Cervantes

Paloma lifted her suitcase onto the bed in her new room, which was painted a bright, cheerful yellow. She felt like a sunflower had swallowed her up, and she liked it. In Kansas, her walls were "barely beige." Paloma's mom had called it a "nice neutral color" that would match everything, but Paloma argued that "barely beige" was a crayon box reject and an insult to flowers and rainbows. At home, she covered the barely beige walls with as many posters as she could.

Sunrise Over Fallujah by Walter Dean Myers

The afternoon sky was dazzling white above the small village. The room we entered was dark and smelly and for a moment I was blinded by the contrast. There were only a few candles lit against one wall. When my eyes became accustomed to the darkness I saw that there were mats lined up along the floor. There were a few women on them, but most of the bodies lying side by side were children.

---

[7] Young students will often shout out suggestions as you write, but it is best if you model a craft move because that is what you want students to do. And admit it, it is fun. Creative work lights up our brains. You don't have to prepare ahead for this. In fact, your model is likely to be better if you struggle a little to find the right words, just as your students do.

1b Reveal and Develop Characters With Sensory Details

FIRST: NOTICE

There are characters who live inside of me. In sixth grade, I bought a notebook so I could be Harriet the Spy in my own neighborhood. I remember peeking under my bed, looking for Ralph S. Mouse and his motorcycle. As Lucy Pevensie aged in *The Chronicles of Narnia*, I imagined who I might become as a hero in my own world. I not only remember those characters, but I also feel who they are—recalling details about them to this day. They shaped many of my beliefs and values. What power reading has on growing minds. The craft moves of the authors shaped my understandings, as did my own rereading of their books.

My devotion to these books came from conditions in my elementary classrooms and in my home. In both places, I had access to books that interested me and time to read them. I lived close to the public library, and my mother took me there almost every week. I adored the Scholastic Book Clubs at school, and I earned money for them by picking strawberries to supplement what my mom could pay out of our strained family finances. My access to books was a privilege that many children still do not have. We must right that imbalance in both classrooms and school libraries.[8]

In the chart on the next page, what do you notice in the passage from *Caged Warrior* on the left? Try to name what Sitomer's sensory details reveal about the character *before you read* "Details I Notice" in the column on the right—as tempting as it may be to jump to my observations. Noticing is not about finding answers; it is about paying close attention to the moves writers make.

---

[8] If you need books, apply for a grant from the Book Love Foundation, which has raised over a million dollars in donations. 100 percent of donations go to teachers who seek to build a love of reading in all students. Read statements from grant recipients and apply at booklovefoundation.org.

Caged Warrior by Alan Sitomer	Details I Notice

Some kids have dads who raise them to be golfers. Others, quarterbacks. Still others to play tennis or soccer or baseball. I was raised to cage fight. Ever since I was three, my dad schooled me to brawl. Taught me to grapple, box, ground-and-pound, strike while standing up, and submit an opponent while lying down. From Sambo to Brazilian jiu-jitsu, Greco-Roman wrestling to Aikido, joint locks to pin holds to pressure-point manipulation, I'm an assassin in the art of hurt. My father wants me to do more than just defeat my opponents; he wants me to destroy them.
 	
    "It's how champions are made," he tells me. "And one day, you will be world champion."
 	
    "Yes, sir."
 	
    How do I feel about all this? Fact is, I don't really give much thought to those kinds of questions. Feelings are luxuries when there's a growl in your family's stomach.
	• There is parallel sentence structure in the opening: *some kids have dads who raise them to be*; *others* (the word *have* is implied); *Still others* (*have* is implied), followed by the contrast: *I was raised to….* This structure sets up a lively, concise description of how he was raised. This is sophisticated sentence work.
	
	• The use of *brawl* as a synonym for *fight* keeps the language interesting instead of needlessly repetitive.
	
	• Verbs are visual: *schooled, grabble, ground-and-pound, strike, submit.* What a perfect passage to launch word study and the process writers use to find lists of synonyms to avoid repetition while writing. Effective vocabulary instruction includes building a personal thesaurus through word collections in notebooks. Help students collect words they'll use, instead of studying obscure words they have no context for.
	
	• Sitomer uses description to inform us; the list of what he was taught to do defines cage fighting.
	
	• Two sentences in close proximity repeat initial sounds: *assassin* in the *art…* and not *defeat…* but *destroy.* This juxtaposition creates a beat—a musicality—in the writing.
	
	• Two lines of dialogue reveal the hierarchy of the relationship between father and son.
	
	• The reflection in the last three sentences brings the reader close to the narrator. We understand a great deal about this character through these details. The narrator also reveals a secret: how he feels about it all. This is an important craft move to establish a connection with the reader; we're now on the same side as our narrator.

SECOND: IMITATE

First, I consider a subject. Sometimes I decide on a subject with students, and sometimes I just begin writing with one in mind.

I speak as I write: "I am going to imitate this passage by focusing on a lesson I learned from my dad. I reread Sitomer's opening sentence: *Some kids have dads who raise them to be golfers.* And I think about my dad teaching me to golf and fish. I could also write about him teaching me tennis or basketball.

But I have written about my dad teaching me things many times before, so I want to try something different today. What did Mom teach me? I make a list to remind myself: to bake perfect pie crust; to make beautifully decorated cookies for the holidays; to always sample the cookies I make before offering them to others; to sew my own clothes.

I have enough to start writing.

I look back at the passage and notice Sitomer starts with something his dad does not teach him to do. And then he describes something he did teach him to do: fight. I'm going to try that."

> *Some kids have moms who pack a briefcase each morning and rush out the door to important jobs. Others sit before a computer and log in to a flood of emails. Still others enter a studio to paint or sculpt or write. My mother taught me to bake.*

I stop and encourage students to get started on their own imitations. Then I go back to writing, even if some students sit before an open notebook watching, not writing. There is a value in watching a teacher write, pause, reread, write again, cross out, add information, and so on. Studying how a writer works is often overlooked, but incredibly valuable.[9] We want our students to be

---

[9] In 2007, I watched Don Murray compose a column for *The Boston Globe* in front of a room of teachers. He spoke about his writing while he worked, crossing out passages and lines as he refined the purpose of his column. When one line led him in a new direction, he sometimes followed it, deleting what came before. After about 10 minutes of his modeling, I realized how ordinary (instead of flawed) my own process was. I often changed subjects once I started or found a more interesting example, even after laboring over another. Here was a Pulitzer Prize-winning writer doing the same. Studying beautiful micro mentor texts sets a bar for young writers. Look at what is possible! When we reveal our struggles as we model, we set another bar: what writers must do to get the work done. It is important to set both bars for students.

in a community of writers, working to make meaning. We are part of that community. As I continue writing, my students see this short text develop:

> Some kids have moms who pack a briefcase each morning and rush out the door to ~~important jobs~~ work. Others, sit before a ~~computer and log in to~~ a flood of email. Still others ~~enter a studio to paint or sculpt or write~~ start the laundry. My mother taught me to bake. Her wooden rolling pin spun side to side and front to back across pale dough spread across a bed of flour. She thinned and pressed the mound of butter and flour to the width of a picture book, then cradled it beneath her hands and flipped it back on the board. A plastic cookie shape cut into the dough, then drowned in a scoop of flour before punching an impression into the dough again. Mom floured and pressed, scooped and rolled, sashaying her hips with the steady rhythm of cookie-making. ~~Making sugary delights brought her joy.~~ There was joy here. I saw her ~~features~~ eyes relax, ~~her~~ a smile sneak across her face, and heard a Sinatra tune whisper into our quiet kitchen. Mom taught me to love creating food and to sample it frequently.

Sitomer's passage led my students to new thinking, which helped them to begin their narrative essays. Here is a student's example.

> Some kids have mothers who bake cookies with them when they come home from school. Some have mothers who sing lullabies as they fall asleep, others don't even have mothers. But I wonder if I had not been adopted if my life with my birthmother would have been filled with Nestle recipes and serenades for slumber.
>
> —Rachel, grade 12

YOUR TURN

Here are five micro mentor texts from beautiful pieces of literature that I have used with students. Each one reveals a character to readers. As I did in the chart in the previous section with the passage from *Caged Warrior*, write what you notice about the writer's craft. This practice fine-tunes your skills in noticing and naming moves and prepares you well for your next lessons.

My dad drops me off at school on his way to the construction site across town, like he does every morning, and before I can jump out of the truck, he puts a hand on my shoulder and does that thing he always does these days, staring so hard at my face I think he might be trying to memorize the number of holes in my skin. Maybe in that quick second, he remembered the way he'd drop my brother off at school, too.

"Have a good day," he says, squeezing my shoulder a little.

"Thank you, sir."

He hesitates, "I love you."

Now, my dad never says those words. I've never heard them come out of his mouth, not once. Never to my mom. Never to my brother. Never to me.

"Waiting"
On Monday
Papi must be late. It's six p.m.
and aftercare closes at six fifteen.
The ticks on the clock
and honey-slow tocks
I try not to count.
I wonder if Papi's broken a wing
on the skyscrapers he helps build
with hammers and steel?
I wonder if Papi forgot
I am waiting and rushed
to the restaurant with too
many dishes to wash?

But that has never happened.
Ms. Cassandra, the teacher's aide,
bends the creases of her forehead
near her phone when Papi doesn't
answer so she calls Mami, who is the
nanny of toddler twins with bright red
cheeks who can't fly.
Ms. Cassandra gives me a tissue
to soak up my teariness because Mami
can't come for me right now either.
She can't leave those babies
until *their* parents get home.
Papi is coming, I whisper to myself.
I'll tuck my wings close and wait.

Me, Frida, and the Secret of the Peacock Ring by Angela Cervantes

She asked where she could find Frida's *My Dress Hangs There* painting. The woman directed her to the first floor. Face-to-face with her father's favorite Frida Kahlo painting, Paloma soaked in the image of Frida's colorful dress dangling from a clothesline in the middle of New York City. All around the dainty dress were New York skyscrapers, Lady Liberty, and images of people marching. Paloma squeezed her eyes shut and imagined herself as the dress, dangling and swaying from a clothesline above the city of Coyoacán.

A soft breeze swept across Paloma's face. She hadn't meant to leave her bedroom window wide open. She peered over her blanket toward a light tinkling noise that reminded Paloma of the wind chimes on her grandparents' porch in Kansas.

Frida Kahlo sat at the vanity. She was dressed in a long green skirt with white ruffles, a red blouse, and a black shawl. Her bracelets clanked and chimed as she pinned a purple flower in her dark hair.

"I'm dreaming again, aren't I?" Paloma asked, sitting up to face the artist.

"*Sí,*" Frida said, flashing Paloma a vibrant smile. "Dreaming is nice, no? But reality is better."

....A tap on the bedroom door startled Paloma awake.

Rick by Alex Gino

"Oh, trust me, Ricky, you're never too busy to take a look at a girl." Sometimes Dad was worse than Jeff. "Or a boy." Mom probably told him to say that part. "You may be a late bloomer, but don't worry, you'll have plenty of time to take in the views, if you know what I mean."

Rick knew what Dad meant, and it made him feel like he was coated in a sticky layer of ick. Rick felt himself sliding down, trying to melt into the chair.

Shadowshaper by Daniel José Older

When Neville smiled, his narrow cheeks seemed to fold into themselves to make room for that great wide mouth.

As you studied these micro mentor texts, you likely noticed that the author brings readers into the minds of characters. We see the world through a character's eyes because of the use of details.[10] These lessons were designed to make students more aware of how writing is crafted, using a range of texts and authors that will ignite their interests.

Noticing and imitating writer's craft are not ends in themselves, however. While we want students to make the leap to noticing writer's craft in the books they have chosen and in the characters with whom they've connected, reading researcher Richard Allington warns, "Reducing a complex activity to a list of key features... is always the risk of oversimplification." Let us not make that mistake. The most important way to support students' growth as readers and writers is by providing access to a wide range of texts they can choose from and read deeply, both inside and outside of school. If we don't make time for students to read books they choose at their own pace, most of them will not develop a love of reading and a desire to apply what we teach them beyond our lessons.

1c Expand a Moment With Sensory Details

FIRST: NOTICE

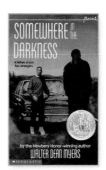

When I am deeply engaged in reading, details often create a movie in my mind. I can feel the engine of a car rumbling beneath my seat; I can feel metal beneath my forearm that hangs lazily out the driver's side window. I hear the radio as the steering wheel spins beneath my hand. Even when I was too young for a driver's license, I could feel details like those while cruising with the characters in *The Outsiders*.

Specific details expand a moment in a story. That moment might include dialogue, either spoken or internal. These

---

[10] You may know of Dr. Rudine Sims Bishop's writing about literature as "windows, mirrors, and sliding glass doors." If you don't, please Google and listen to an interview with her at #WeNeedDiverseBooks.

details work together to slow down time and expand the moment. Sometimes details bring the reader into the setting with the character, noticing what the character notices, taking it all in.

How do writers expand a moment? Answering that question is the focus of this section—and students will learn to use that craft move in fiction and nonfiction, throughout their years in school.[11] Writers use clear, specific details to expand moments.

What do you notice in the passage on the left, in the following chart? Remember, try to name a few craft moves *before you read* "Details I Notice" in the column on the right. Trust your analytical skills. You will see many details in this passage.

Somewhere in the Darkness by Walter Dean Myers	Details I Notice
Some more people came into the diner. They were working people and mostly black. One man was tall with a long neck. He wore a belt with tools on it. Jimmy tried to figure out what he did. There were three different kinds of pliers on the broad leather belt he wore, all with red handles, a few screwdrivers, and one tool that Jimmy had never seen before. The man straddled a stool as if it were a horse and started reading his newspaper. The man who had taken their order brought the tall man coffee and a doughnut without exchanging words with him.	• The observation moves from general (some people) to specific (one man). This mimics the way we might scan a room and then settle on one person. • Myers is showing us who Jimmy is by what Jimmy sees. Jimmy is observant. He collects details to determine what this man does or to understand who the people are that come here. • He spends 30 words describing the tool belt. I wonder why. • The last two sentences show a cowboy— which implies grace and strength. We learn that the man is a reader. And we see he must be a regular customer because the waiter knows what he wants without asking him.

We know that the extent to which a student comprehends a text depends largely on background knowledge. Considering that, Myers assumes his reader knows what a diner looks like. I do because I worked at one. I see a long

---

[11] Vignettes might open an essay or feature article that argues for a cause, such as funding of an arts program.

counter and stools, plus booths and tables spread throughout. The kitchen is behind the counter with a pass-through window. I imagine a glass coffee pot in the hand of a waitress, just like the one I used to carry.

However, I'm certain that many of my students will not conjure that image when they see the word *diner*. Should I stop and teach this word to them? As I look at the rest of the passage, I realize students don't need to know this word to understand what is happening. Myers gives them enough information to know that a diner is a place where food is served, and that is information enough to understand the passage.

SECOND: IMITATE

Try the move with me.

I need a person to observe and write about as I plan my week's lessons. It's a perfect time of day for a latte, so I take my notebook to a coffee shop in town. My New Hampshire town attracts many tourists, and they provide me with rich material for writing. If you don't want to travel, consider opening an Internet browser and searching for "photos of interesting people." You'll find plenty of images to use for this practice in class.

→ TIP

Encourage Students to Be Word Collectors

If you want to create students who are curious about words they don't know, have them collect those words in a notebook. We want students to leave each school year having done a lot of reading because the more they read, the more words they learn and have at their disposal as writers.[12]

[12] As author, editor, and educator Lois Bridges said, "Reading engagement is nothing short of miraculous. Engaged readers spend 500 percent more time reading than do their peers who aren't turned on by books—and all those extra hours inside books they love gives them a leg up in everything that leads to a happy, productive life: *deep conceptual understanding* about a wide range of topics, *expanded vocabulary*, strategic reading ability, critical literacy skills, and engagement with the world that's more likely to make them dynamic citizens drawn into full civic participation" (italics mine).

I return to Myers's passage. I use his opening lines to get myself thinking as I scan the coffee shop and begin listing images. In class the next day, I develop this writing in front of students.

Although we often tell stories in past tense, readers enter them more easily when they're written in present tense, I tell my students. Readers want to be in the moment with the writer.

> *A small crowd enters through the front door. They have bags bulging with packages.*

I stop and explain my thinking to students, "As I wrote about the crowd, I found a phrase I liked because of the sound of the repeated 'b' and 'g' in 'bags bulging with packages'." I read the sentence aloud so students can hear what I mean. But when I reread it, I don't like '*had bags*,' so I replace the passive verb *have* with the active verb *carry*. I want readers to see this moment as I'm seeing it—moving.

> *A small crowd enters through the front door. They ~~had~~ carry bags bulging with packages.*

I continue, "Now I will follow Myers' example by moving from the general (a crowd) to the specific (a shopper)." I read aloud the first two sentences and keep going.

> *A small crowd enters through the front door. They carry bags bulging with packages. One woman is wearing boots with tall heels. She stretches up on her toes, then back down, as if her feet are sore. She carries bags from many stores, one set of handles inside the next. After placing her order, she drops the bags in a heap beside her to reach for her wallet. One bag topples over, spilling sweaters and a water bottle and a tiny wooden firetruck onto the tile floor. She glances from the floor to the barista and says, "I'll take a chocolate chip cookie as well." They both giggle as she hands over her credit card.*

YOUR TURN

Select one of the following passages that you feel is a good fit for your students and use it to demonstrate expanding a moment, as I did in the last section. Notice I include another passage from *King and the Dragonflies*. Using it would be a great way to extend the learning from Craft Move 1a on revealing setting with sensory details.

King and the Dragonflies by Kacen Callender

...there's a crunching behind me. I turn and look to see a rusting white pickup coming, kicking up dust behind it, so I step to the side of the road and onto the browning grass, expecting it to zoom by, but the pickup slows down until it stops right beside me. There's a few white boys inside, but my heart drops into my stomach when I see the driver. Mikey Sanders...He's got a sunburn across his face and tiny blue eyes and pale hair, so pale it might as well be white, too. He's smoking a cigarette even though I know he isn't yet eighteen, and he wears a collared shirt like he's just come back from church...Mikey Sanders is here, looking at me like he's thinking of dragging me from the back of his pickup truck, too. He doesn't say anything for a long moment. Just looks me up and down, his truck's engine still rumbling and shaking, almost as much as I'm trembling on my feet. His friends in the passenger seat and the back seat are as silent as stones. Mikey flicks his cigarette to the ground and sucks on his teeth. I flinch, and I know how I must look to him. I look scared—like I'm about to wet my pants.

Rick by Alex Gino

"I'll miss you too," said Diane, as though it were a challenge. They entangled in a mess of long straight black hair and pale pink limbs. Dad joined in with his thicker, hairier arms and wavy light brown hair, and called Rick into the family huddle. Rick had Dad's hair and Mom's skin tone, but sometimes, like most kids, he wondered where he had come from.

Pong had never thought about escaping Namwon before, but now the opportunity lurched up like a mudskipper[13] and slapped him across the face with its tail. He could get out of Namwon. Not when he was thirteen. *Now.*

Without pausing to think, Pong tipped the basket and climbed inside. He took one last gulp of semi-fresh air and wriggled down under the trash. He nearly threw up as he pushed the durian[14] skins, orange rinds, and banana peels up around him, packing them over his head, covering his face.

He breathed through his mouth as shallowly as he could. With one eye pressed against the straw weave of the basket, he could see a blurry, golden view of what was happening outside.

He froze when he heard footsteps coming closer. Someone swung open the basket lid and held it open for a long time. Pong listened but couldn't tell who stood there. Somkit? A guard? Whoever it was, they shut the lid and walked away.

Surely Somkit would wonder where he'd gone. Surely he would start asking if anyone had seen Pong. But no one called for him. And Somkit never came back.

Pong sat gagging in the basket, stinky juice dripping off his hair and down the bridge of his nose. He didn't know if he could make it until the trashman came back. The whole thing began to feel like a really bad idea.

Their Turn: Independent Practice

Independent practice is an essential move that anchors the learning of a craft move. Guided practice in noticing details and in using them to enliven writing is important, but we want students to gather their own collections of micro mentor texts. Sometimes we underestimate what students can do. A student may find weak examples (in your mind) of sensory details… a yellow dress, a wilted flower, for example. But if that student has never thought about elements of writer's craft before, this is an important first step. I think of independent practice on a continuum. First simple examples; soon more layered, complex, vivid ones.

---

[13] I would show students a picture of a mudskipper. After all, it's difficult to imagine this moment without a visual. And mudskippers are both interesting and kind of disgusting!

[14] Oh my… the smell of durian will never leave you once you've inhaled it. It is considered the most foul-smelling fruit in the world and has even been *banned* from public spaces in Singapore.

Students will learn a great deal from each other. When they gather to share beautiful examples of writer's craft, they will also share a love of and a curiosity about words and passages that ignite energy for both reading and writing.

When studying this craft move, I ask students to collect passages that contain rich sensory details and put them into categories in their writer's notebooks, which helps them organize information not only on the page, but also in their brains. So many things happen at once when we read a story: We are getting to know the characters; we see where they live and what it is like to live there; we feel tension as the events gather momentum; we notice the role of minor characters. A collecting sheet is designed to slow down the reader to pay closer attention to craft moves that the author uses to reveal details.

I create a collecting sheet in front of students. I have a section for each of the five senses because that is the craft move we are currently studying.[15] I show students how sensory details can be collected in categories. This will help me focus on what I notice as I read.

The collecting sheet has open sections to be named and filled in by students. When I begin, I'm not sure what I'll notice, so I leave the sections blank. The blank sections allow students to find and name other interesting craft moves.

This freedom is critical to developing students' independence. My goal is to have students practice noticing sensory details, but I also hope they will discover alliteration or personification or fascinating similes. One fifth grader I worked with kept track of the names of characters to see whether there was a pattern to them; another started a list of chapter titles to see whether there was a theme or a preview of what was to come. One fifth grader created an "interesting comparisons" category because he was noticing such comparisons occurring in his book. I celebrate what students notice in this independent practice; I can create an anchor chart of categories students are discovering.

TIP

Create a Listening Station

What if I have students who are struggling to read the text we've chosen to study? I set up a listening station with the audiobook. Students can follow the text, pausing to record passages and craft moves that they find meaningful.

---

[15] In the center, I create a drawing inspired by the book's cover because I enjoy sketching. Your students might, too.

I begin with a blank spread, and over the coming days I add descriptive passages that use sensory details. Some days I read a passage aloud and then add it to the blank chart under the document camera. Other days I fill in passages before class and have students read them as they arrive to class. I collect passages over several days, reminding students of the ongoing nature of this work.

Each spread should be the student's own. You may find some students so busy finding sensory details that they do not write them down on their collecting sheets. When I notice that happening, I redirect students to record what they see, with suggestions such as, "Oh, write that down! I love that," or "I would like to add that passage to my collecting sheet. Is that okay with you? Can you leave your notebook for me at the end of work time, so I can copy this passage?" The generative nature of this activity allows students to build on what they know. One student may not notice any details of smell, while another focuses only on them. When students gather in pairs and small groups to share what they have found, their understanding of writer's craft grows based on their individual differences and interests.

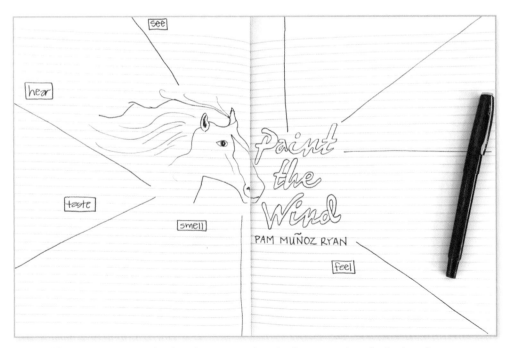

A spread from my writing notebook to demonstrate how I collect examples of writer's craft

But wait!

Not too much.

Please, not every book.

We want students to get lost in their reading.

We *also* want students to make meaningful discoveries of writer's craft.

Those two goals can work together, but not if this leads to skimming a book simply to find something to record in their notebooks. You will see the difference as you watch students work.

You know you want to get started on your own collection, right?

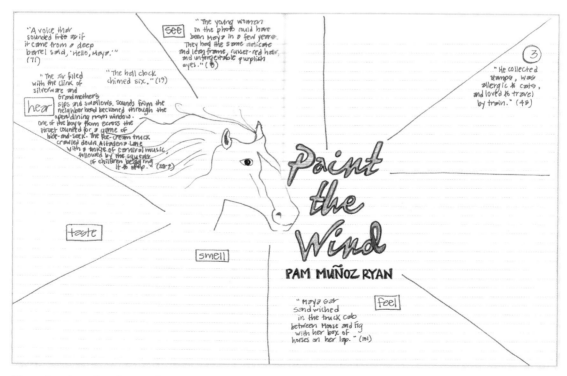

After a few days of work, my collection is growing. You'll notice that I've added my own category "3," where I introduce students to the idea that three examples give a sentence a certain symmetry. This is a preview of work we will soon focus on together—organizing artfully: the power of three.

Chapter 2

Organizing Artfully: The List

"The great thing about coming of age as a writer in Chicago is that you have a skyscrapered, schoolyarded, L train-tracked electricity in each space you sprawl into—a checkerboard of ethnicities to navigate and explore all the American tongues. In Chicagoland, poets inhabit the XY axes of gridded streets to teach you that if the poem is gonna be worth it, it better sneak sweat-close to your skin and snatch off your chains."

—Tyehimba Jess, from *Respect the Mic: Celebrating 20 Years of Poetry from a Chicagoland High School*

We often rely on lists of information to understand something complex. For example, we study the features of an apartment we are looking to rent or the balance of ingredients in Mom's pie crust. When we consider *artful* ways to organize, we think about order of items. Consider that apartment. There are two bedrooms, two bathrooms, wood floors, and new cabinets, but also a shaded patio with a view to the city! A good writer does not bury the patio in the list of bedrooms and bathrooms. He emphasizes it by placing it at the end of the list.

Once you begin to notice this craft move, you will see it everywhere.[16] For example, there are list poems ("21" by Patrick Roche and "10 Reasons Why Fathers Cry at Night" by Kwame Alexander), travel guides ("10 Must-See Museums in Rome" and "The 50 Best Places for Chicken Wings"), movie reviews ("Ways the *Game of Thrones* Finale Disappointed Viewers"), essays ("You May Want to Marry My Husband" by Amy Krouse Rosenthal), reports (CNN's "What Would Make You Care About Aleppo?").

In the introduction to her wonderful poetry collection, *Falling Down the Page: A Book of List Poems,* Georgia Heard describes a setting with a short list of observations:

> Out for a walk in New York City I see: yellow cabs speeding down Broadway; people lounging in over-stuffed chairs at a coffee shop. I hear: cars honking; a dog barking in the distance. As I walk along I make a list in my head of what I observe just like Walt Whitman did over one hundred years ago in his famous list poem *Song of Myself*. (2009)

[16] The List is a craft move that authors of informational books use all the time, including me. I considered the order of craft moves in my table of contents (a list of big ideas) to communicate the importance of them individually and collectively. I move from the easiest-to-spot craft moves (e.g., sensory details) to more sophisticated ones (e.g., literary devices).

You might begin a study of this craft move with a walk. Take students on a tour of the neighborhood or the halls of the school and ask them to make a list of what they notice. Model this by stopping occasionally and expressing what you notice. *I hear the silence in the auditorium and see rows of shadowed seats when no one is here.* When you return to class, collect the observations and write a class poem. Model how sensory details add depth to the list. After all, craft moves ideally work together, reinforcing one another.

If a tour is not possible, *imagine* going on one together and list what students notice in their minds. What do they see when they imagine a walk from the classroom to the buses after school? When they travel with their grandparents to church? When they ride a skateboard from the steps of their apartments across the city streets to a park?

TWO IMPORTANT POINTS

Students need to remember two important points about creating lists:

1. Be selective. Writers include what they believe is important and exclude what they believe isn't because it distracts from their focus. In a description of a character, the writer might include one or more details that truly capture what she feels is important for readers to know about that character and exclude or limit others. She decides what to include *and* what to leave out.

Here's an example from the luminous *The Moon Within* by Aida Salazar.[17] Celi, the main character, describes the music of her house as she waits to fall asleep:

> I smile to think that specks of dust
>   dance around me
> though I don't hear music.
> Maybe they dance to the clicks and creaks
> of our little house in Oakland
>   and the city crickets
>   and Mima's and Papi's footsteps
>   outside my door
>   JuJu's steady breathing.

---

[17] Seriously. The language in this book is so gentle. It is like listening to the loons call across the lake as I sit writing this morning. It breathes. You are awash in images. You simply *must* order this book for yourself and your young writers. It is an important addition to your library.

We can see Celi in her bed listening, wondering, while we marvel at her list of details: *dust particles*; *clicks and creaks*; *footsteps*; *breathing*. Her list moves from the details of her house to the people in it, from sight to sounds. Such a range! But we know there is plenty she *doesn't* include here. Writers are selective.

2. Write beautifully about ordinary things. Too many young writers feel they need a big idea and a big event to write. When you show an example such as Aida Salazar's, you show how she uses the beauty of language to craft an everyday moment in her house.

2a Describe Characters Using a List

FIRST: NOTICE

In the following chart, in the column on the left, is a short passage from *King and the Dragonflies* by Kacen Callender.

What do you notice in the passage? Try to name a few craft moves *before you read* "Details I Notice" in the column I've filled in on the right.

King and the Dragonflies by Kacen Callender	Details I Notice
The dragonflies live down by the bayou, but there's no way to know which one's my brother. I've never seen so many dragonflies around this time of the year. There are hundreds, maybe even thousands, just sitting on tree branches and rocks, baking in the sun, flitting over the	• This is the opening of the book, which is one reason it is so powerful. We see the central idea in one complex sentence: King believes the spirit of his brother has been reborn as a dragonfly. We know our central character is grieving and looking for his brother in an insect. He believes in an afterlife. Not many novels deliver so much information in a sentence. It makes me want to search a stack in my library and make a list of first lines. • We get a feel for King's powers of observation as he notices many dragonflies, then lists what they do.

King and the Dragonflies continued	Details I Notice
brown water that seeps up from the dirt, zipping across the sky, showing off their ghostlike wings. Happy in their dragonfly paradise.	• Callender personifies dragonflies: *showing off their ghostlike wings.* • *Ghostlike* is an echo; it reminds us that the spirit of his brother is in a dragonfly. • The final description *happy* echoes the two earlier verbs: *flitting, zipping.* These are carefree words. It makes me wonder whether King is using them because he is trying to imagine his brother is happy in his new life.

SECOND: IMITATE

This example is built on observation. I imagine being in my kitchen, I tell students. I glance around for something to focus on. My corgi is asleep on the floor beside me. To begin my description, I look back at Callender's passage from *King and the Dragonflies* for a starting place.

> *Julius springs awake when he hears the coffee pot beep. He grumbles low in his throat and glances around, then slowly puts his head back on the rug.*

I continue writing in front of students, stopping to tell them that I want to imitate Callender's list of actions with interesting verbs like the author used (*sitting, baking, flitting, zipping*). I will try their craft move of describing a character with a list.

> *When I stand to refill my mug, Julius springs from the floor, follows me to the counter, and barks. His eyes track mine, his tail sweeps back and forth, and his front and back legs dance, as he waits for me to say, "Walk?"*

 TIP

Don't Limit "Imitation" to the Classroom

To connect the practice of writing in class to the practice of writing outside of class, I often start an imitation at home or in a coffee shop and then continue working on it in front of students— suggesting they do the same!

I lean on the structure of the passage further.[18] I am disappointed that my imitation has none of the beauty and tranquility of Callender's passage, so I pay attention to how the author's words evoke those feelings, and then turn my attention to my own descriptive writing. These are important moves for any writer to practice.

FIRST: NOTICE SOME MORE

Yes, I'm sharing two passages, with "Details I Notice," before I give you others to study. Why? I just love both passages so much! I think of you sitting beside me and my annoying habit of asking, *What about this? And this? Oh, and look at this!* I get pretty excited talking about writer's craft.

Zac & Mia by A. J. Betts	Details I Notice
Mum's not a four-wall kind of woman. As long as I can remember, she's always had a straw hat and a sheen of sweat. She's hazel eyes and sun spots. She's greens and browns and oranges. She's a pair of pruning shears in hand. She's soil and pumpkins. She'd rather be picking pears or fertilizing olive trees than stuck in this room, with its pink reclining chair. More than	• The first sentence is a claim about what the character's mother is not. • There is parallel structure in *a straw hat and a sheen of sweat*, and then *hazel eyes and sun spots*. The parallel pattern is adjective-noun, and, adjective-noun. • Three colors represent Mum, and the series items are connected by *and* instead of commas. The beat of the sentence is different with the connecting word *and*. I would suggest it is more musical than a list containing items separated by commas. • *A pair of pruning shears in hand* conveys her love of gardening, followed by naming her with two nouns (*soil* and *pumpkins*) that strengthen this image.

[18] Students can imitate in their notebooks, adhering closely to an author's form and ideas, to practice how well-written lists are created. They don't *have to* adhere to Callender's writing, but many of them likely will. If students imitate an author's writing very closely in their own writing beyond their notebook, be sure they cite the author and source. We teach students what it means to give credit by reinforcing the importance of naming where our ideas come from.

Zac & Mia continued	Details I Notice
anything, she's my dad's soul mate, though she won't go home when I ask her—even when I beg her.	• The last list of attributes contains another parallel: *picking pears or fertilizing olive trees* (verb, noun, verb, noun) focusing on her activity outdoors—echoing the opening claim: *not a four-wall kind of woman.* The contrast that follows—she is *stuck in this room* beside her son—shows how he recognizes her love. • The last line contains another claim: *my dad's soul mate.* • The use of the dash and aside at the end—*even when I beg her*—reveals the voice and desperation of this narrator.

SECOND: IMITATE

The first time I used Betts's passage with students, I had just returned from a Taylor Swift concert with my daughter. I put a picture from the concert on the screen as they arrived, inviting small talk as I took attendance and waited for the bell. To start class, I projected the passage from *Zac & Mia* and quickly summarized why students might want to add this book to their "next" list of titles, at the back of their writing notebooks. This is a quick book talk, designed to help students find books they want to read next. As they read, I conferred with a few, and then I brought them back to the passage to begin our daily writing in notebooks.

I showed another picture of Taylor Swift that my daughter took that night. "So, you all know her, right?" I asked. Students nodded. (And some rolled their eyes.) "I want you and a partner to stand on the shoulders of A. J. Betts and imitate her writing to describe Ms. Swift. You might start like this:

> *Taylor is not a four-wall kind of woman. As long as I can remember, she's always had..."*

And I paused, inviting students to offer phrases—*lots of boyfriends, red lipstick, high heels.* We laughed. I ask them to get into pairs and write about someone nearby, imitating Betts's craft move as I did. After a few minutes, I let one student read her description and then asked others to offer alternatives for each line. Students were wildly and effectively creative in their imitations, as you can imagine.

I recorded their ideas on chart paper, which I left hanging at the front of class. When the next class came in, they could see what I was up to. This class happened to be filled with eleventh-grade boys who were hunters, fishers, and avowed country kids. Will said, "Oh no, if we're doing this, we ain't using Taylor. Give us Garth or..." and I did.

> *Garth Brooks is not a four-wall kind of man. As long as I can remember, he's always had...*

During the imitation phase, get creative about grouping. Sometimes have everyone practice alone, sometimes in pairs, sometimes as a class. It's all practice, after all, and it elevates thinking about writer's craft.

BONUS!

Connect this imitation lesson to students' independent reading. Have them choose one character in a book they are reading. In notebooks, ask them to write a description of one character by imitating Betts's description. You can model this using a character from a book you're reading. (If students are in book clubs, have them collaborate on a character. They will deepen their thinking discussing the character and seeing the character through the eyes of each book club member.)[19]

YOUR TURN

You know your students better than I do. Select one of the following passages that you feel is a good fit for your students and use it to demonstrate using a list to describe a character, as I did in the last section.

---

[19] Don't you love how malleable this work is? I bet your brain is buzzing with possibilities.

The Paperboy by Dav Pilkey	*The Great Gracie Chase* by Cynthia Rylant
His dog, too, knows this route by heart. He knows which trees are for sniffing. He knows which birdbaths are for drinking, which squirrels are for chasing, and which cats are for growling at.	Once there was a little round dog named Gracie Rose. She was a very good dog. She helped the bigger dog watch the house. She kept the kitty company. She even sang to the fish when it was lonely.

2b Describe Settings Using a List

FIRST: NOTICE

In the chart on the next page, in the column on the left, is a short passage from *Rhythm Ride* by Andrea Davis Pinkney. When describing a setting, authors most often pay attention to what they see and hear. Details of smell are unusual, so they are particularly effective. Also, notice how details work to create a sense of place. The description will invite you to linger or convince you to flee.

What do you notice in the passage? Try to name a few craft moves *before you read* "Details I Notice" in the column I've filled in to the right of the passage. It's tempting to just jump to my observations, isn't it? But this practice we are doing is not about finding answers; it is about practicing paying close attention to the moves writers make.

Rhythm Ride by Andrea Davis Pinkney	Details I Notice
Berry and his family hung a sign out front that immediately caught the attention of anyone who passed by. Neighbors looked at the sign and wondered what would come out of that house. When young mothers wheeled their babies by in strollers, the toddlers who saw those bold blue letters did a double take. Even dogs out for a walk and stray cats trying to find their way home took notice of Berry's sign. It was a sign of the times. It was Berry's make-no-mistake intention. It said: HITSVILLE U.S.A.	• At first, we don't know what the sign says, but as we read the list of how others react when they see it, we know the sign says something important or surprising. • Each item in the list is not only its own sentence, but also its own paragraph. • The last example of dogs seems to build on the sentence before. It must be something if toddlers notice, but Andrea piles on with *even dogs take notice.* • There is subject-verb agreement: Neighbors *looked,* mothers *wheeled* babies and toddlers *did a double take,* and even dogs and stray cats *noticed.* • Consider the order of who notices the sign: first neighbors, then young mothers walking by, then babies, toddlers, and even dogs and cats. Why this order?

SECOND: IMITATE

By giving a list of how the sign draws attention, what is Pinkney hoping readers will infer about it? Perhaps that others beyond those mentioned might have noticed the sign? I would say to students, How about *policemen on the night shift driving by* or *a Little League team coming home from a game?* We could make a list together of possibilities. This sends a message that, quite often, writers imagine lots of possibilities and then choose the ones that show best what they are trying to communicate. They don't use them all because the story would likely lose momentum. (Another important lesson for young writers: The delete key is your friend.)

What if I arrived at school on Monday and the entire building had been painted purple? I might have students turn and talk to come up with a list of ways to show the impact of this change by describing the reactions of those who see

it: parents bringing kids to school, the principal, the teachers, the students....
Then consider the order in which to put those reactions. Have students share
their lists and explain why they believe they should be ordered that way.

As we studied Pinkney's passage together, students asked: "Why put these
three examples in this order? Why put neighborhood pets last?"

I offered a guess: "I would say that pets came last because it is unlikely that
pets notice most signs on the street. Other ideas?"

A student said, "Andrea used it to make readers smile because anyone who
reads the book knows how playful she is."

I celebrated her answer and added, "We can't know. I love that about this
study. There is no right answer.[20] Writers always make decisions. Authors
create—just like you." Imitating craft moves is a catalyst to get writers' minds
spinning with ideas.

YOUR TURN

Select one of the following micro mentor texts that you feel is a good fit for
your students. Notice there is a house, a car, a laundry room, and a group
house. Or put all four on chart paper or the whiteboard and ask students to
select one to study in a group. Ask them to gather around the text and talk
through what they notice, leaving notes for a group share. Use these micro
mentor texts to study how authors use a list of specific details to describe a
setting, as I did in the last section.

Illegal **by Francisco X. Stork**

The houses that lined the street all had the same basic design. Two-story houses with
a garage, a driveway, front yard and backyard. There was space between the houses,
not like in my neighborhood back home, where I could stick my hand out the kitchen
window and get a warm tortilla from Mrs. Lozano next door. The major difference
between the houses here, beside their size and good condition, was their subdued
colors, as if people were afraid to call attention to themselves.

---

[20] So much learning has been hijacked by the practice of asking students to find right answers to pass
tests. When we study craft moves, we free students to imagine an author at work and come up with
their own theories for decisions authors make.

Illegal by Francisco X. Stork

In Brother Patricio's beat-up Toyota, the hot air from the open windows was more real. There were smells back then: roadkill, burning brush, the magical odor of eucalyptus appearing out of nowhere. The only smell inside the van was my father's cologne, a mixture of alcohol and something flowery that was making me nauseous.[21]

*

There was a washing machine, a dryer, a small tool bench, and a table with clothes neatly folded. Next to it was the hot water heater and a furnace connected with pipes to the ceiling. There was a stationary bicycle and a rowing machine and behind there was a single bed with one of those goose-feathers quilts that Sara and I had once thought of buying for Mami but couldn't because they were so expensive. The only light in the room came from a small window at the top of the dryer.

Of Mice and Men by John Steinbeck

The bunk house was a long, rectangular building inside, the walls whitewashed and the floor unpainted. In three walls there were small, square windows, and in the fourth, a solid door with a wooden latch. Against the walls were eight bunks, five of them made up with blankets and the other three showing their burlap ticking. Over each bunk there was nailed an apple box with the opening forward so that it made two shelves for the personal belongings of the occupant of the bunk. And these shelves were loaded with little articles, soap and talcum powder, razors, and those Western magazines ranch men love to read and scoff at and secretly believe. And there were medicines on the shelves, and little vials, combs; and from nails on the box sides, a few neckties. Near one wall there was a black cast-iron stove, its stovepipe going straight up through the ceiling. In the middle of the room stood a big square table littered with playing cards, and around it were grouped boxes for the players to sit on.

The Living by Matt de la Peña

He shoved debris out of his way: splintered paintings, fall statues, potted plants, jagged shards of shattered mirrors, chunks of the ceiling and the walls and the stairs. Empty life jackets. Motionless bodies.

---

[21] Smell is a neglected sensory detail. So, try focusing on it exclusively with your students.

In his classroom in Anaheim, California, Kelly Gallagher used the Steinbeck example for notebook practice. One of his students wrote this:

> The 6 trains are rectangular cars linked together, making a silver metal sausage, with the decal number 6 on the side rectangular windows of the cars. Inside, the baby blue seats line both sides of the car, above a black and white speckled floor. People sit opposite each other, sleeping, gazing off into space, or silently wondering about the lives and problems of their fellow passengers. Metal poles are strategically placed through the middle of the car, giving standing passengers a place to grab. Above the seats hang advertisements for sleazy lawyers or television shows, many of which are inappropriate for the youngsters on the train. After repeated stops, the car fills, becoming so crowded that the floors and windows are no longer visible.

Can't you see a wall in your classroom, the school library, or a hallway filled with such rich examples from your students?

2c Describe Actions Using a List

FIRST: NOTICE

In the following chart, in the column on the left, is a short passage from *The Great Greene Heist* by Varian Johnson, which has wonderful energy. The characters move, and in this study, we look at how a series of movements (a list) affects readers.

What do you notice in the passage? Try to name a few craft moves *before you read* "Details I Notice" in the column I've filled in to the right of the passage.

The Great Greene Heist by Varian Johnson	Details I Notice

Or maybe he could just forge a pass from the main office. Slip out of class. Pick the lock and sneak into the teachers' lounge. He knew all about the Hershey's bars Coach Rainey hid behind the sacks of dust-coated Styrofoam cups. The extra ham and Swiss sandwich Mr. James, the security guard, always packed for a tight afternoon snack. The box of mocha-caramel cupcakes Assistant Principal Nelson brought for the Junior National Honor Society's "Welcome Back" social.
 	
    It would have been easy. So easy.
 	
    Jackson pushed these thoughts out of his head. It was only September. He refused to jeopardize four months of model behavior for a quick snack, no matter how hungry he was. No matter how simple it would be.
 	
    No matter how much the idea tingled his spine.
 	
    He paused at the door and glanced at the Gaby De La Cruz for President poster, her name in big, bold, loopy letters. His fingers tightened around the note in his pocket.
	• When we see a character in action, the verbs (*wove, forge, slip, pick, sneak*) show us how he moved. Sometimes I highlight this craft move by substituting other verbs (*crept, steal, sprint, break, burst*) into the same sentences and have students discuss how it changes their perception of the character.
	
	• As we follow the character's actions, we also hear his inner thoughts. Both reveal who this character is.
	
	• Our character is a powerful, precise observer of other characters. Focus on all he knows about the staff from his observations listed in the first paragraph.
	
	• In the first paragraph, *he could* is followed by an action. In the two fragments that follow, *he could* is not stated, but carried in the reader's mind. We could call these "incomplete sentences," but they function as complete thoughts. This distinction is important because students will often find this craft move in books they read.
	
	• One way to name the role a person has is to set it off in commas: *Mr. James, the security guard, always packed…*.
	
	• Here is an opportunity to study paragraphs. Ask students to imagine why the author decided to make one sentence or two into their own paragraphs. What impact does that have on reading?[22]
	
	• Look at the sensory impact in one phrase: *the idea tingled his spine.*

[22] It is not wise to teach students that a paragraph always has a certain number of sentences, considering authors do not follow that rule. If we want students to learn about writing from their reading, we must celebrate the malleability of writer's craft. Punctuation is a convention, as is paragraph structure. Both are elements of style.

The Great Greene Heist continued	Details I Notice
When he reached the garden he moved the note to his shirt pocket, then peeled off his blazer and folded it across the wood fence.	• There is parallel *sentence* structure in the repetition of *no matter how*. • Notice how carefully the character treats his jacket. What does this say about him?

SECOND: IMITATE

When engaged in a craft study, my students and I try to wrap our minds around what authors are doing as they write. Often, as a result, exquisite craft appears as we revise.

Just deciding on a subject and bringing it alive is a challenge. It has become easier for me from the daily practice of modeling my thinking and writing—and most importantly, my rereading and revising—with students, day after day. It will become easier for you as well.

My first decision: fiction or nonfiction? I find it easier to take someone I know (a friend, my dog) and imagine them moving in a setting. I can fictionalize a particular moment, using my knowledge of that person (or animal) to drive the writing.

Today, I decide to write about my best friend, Yukari, and I look back at Varian's writing to get started. His passage begins with a verb phrase, so I imitate that.

> *Zipping her jacket all the way to her throat, Yukari shakes off a shiver and bounces in place.*[23] *She smiles and turns toward the street as I join her. She cuts the corner, brushing against a hydrangea, and glances at the walk sign ahead. It pulses: 8... 7... 6.... She sprints through the intersection, then slows down to a fast walk on the other*

---

[23] I see her in the parking lot outside our rented condo on a recent trip. Although this moment did not happen on this trip, it did on other trips to coffee shops we've taken. I'm using the details I know about Yukari to construct this imitation, and I let students know that so they feel free to imagine people they know in moments that may not have happened but could have. This practice sharpens our observational skills.

side. Her shoes are pristine, double-knotted in symmetrical loops.[24]
Her stride lengthens as she begins talking. She darts around an
elderly man and his tiny dog without a word.

We arrive at a coffee shop to find a line of customers stretching out
the door and onto the sidewalk. Yukari leans to one side and then
the other, judging the time it will take before we can order, as she
continues talking. A former vice president for several tech start-ups,
she has little time for delay.

When I invite students to reread their writing and revise it, I underline the verbs
I've used to describe Yukari's actions. Are they precise? Accurate? Vivid? Can
I think of better verbs? I also look back at our micro mentor text to name and
imitate another craft move: there is parallel structure in several sentences
because of the repetition of the phrase *no matter how*. I will try that.

No matter how brisk the weather, Yukari will sprint for coffee. No
matter how long the line, she'll wait. No matter how bad the brew,
she'll drink it.

That was fun! I smile as I write the last line. I believe students should see joy in
teaching and writing. Don Graves taught me that students learn why people
write from how their teacher approaches writing. Our modeling is about so
much more than showing how to construct sentences.[25]

YOUR TURN

There are *many* good choices to study with students on the next few pages.
Surely you will find one that is a good fit for your students. Use one or more to
demonstrate using a list to describe actions, as I did in the last section.

---

[24] As I reread this sentence, the passive verb (*are*) bothers me. I could rewrite this sentence along these
lines: *As her stride lengthens, the double-knotted symmetrical loops of laces bounce off her pristine
shoes.* I might cross out that sentence out in revision, though, because it's too complicated. But I like
to give myself options and to model for students that I can always play with how I say something.

[25] "How a teacher acts can impact the way a student learns. An educator who expresses, even through
body language, a reluctance with a given subject…gives off a powerful message. Attitude, as it's
been said, is everything." ~Lauren Black, summarizing a Stanford University study

The Dreamer by Pam Muñoz Ryan

Grateful to be released, Neftalí slid from his chair and ran to his room. There, with the muffled voices of the grown-ups in the background, he paused before his collections. He straightened the rows of rocks, twigs, and nests, touching each item as if taking attendance. Father's words echoed.

Absentminded. Absentminded.

It did not make sense. How could he be absentminded when his head was so crowded with thoughts?

He opened the drawer and unfolded each piece of paper he had saved. Then he read the words, mouthing each one perfectly. Before he replaced them, he added one more: *luma*.

Later, as he lay in bed, Neftalí tried to imagine the beetle on the *luma* tree, the one that looked like a living jewel and could disappear in the blink of an eye.

Father's words haunted him.

Neftalí wished that time would disappear as fast as the colorful beetle—in one poof—so he, too, could discover what would become of him.

Countdown by Deborah Wiles

I drain the bathtub, brush my teeth, and put on my pajamas. I pad down the hallway with Jo Ellen's letter, walk straight to her hope chest, and tug on the top, in case it might be unlocked. It isn't, and Mom still hasn't asked me about the key. Nobody can think of everything at a time like this, not even Mom.

I take myself back to my bedroom as the rain pours down outside. I stare at that Ebenezer address on the envelope. That's all it says. Ebenezer. There is no postmark. No stamp. I am officially stumped.

Even Nancy Drew is stumped from time to time. I slide the letter under my mattress. I miss my sister. If she were here, I could sit next to her when we watch President Kennedy, and she could tell me everything would be all right. I would believe her.

***

We are glued to the television as a family, at seven o-clock. Mom and Dad sit on the couch. Uncle Otts is in his chair. Drew and I are there with Jack, on the floor, in our pajamas and slippers, in the same positions we take when we watch Walt Disney's Wonderful World of Color, only there is no Tinker Bell, no Walt Disney, no thrilling opening music.

When I walked in, my ma was washing dishes on the dining room table, pouring water from a kettle into the rinse pan. Usually she did this with the overhead light on, filling the room with light—one of her few luxuries. We weren't supposed to turn that light on unless necessary.[26]

*

I looked at the places where our walls were covered with plastic stapled to insulation, and at the newspaper under the water pail where we kept drinking water from the hand pump outside—to say nothing of the slop pail in the corner. I heard a dog nosing in the closed-off kitchen at the back, where part of the roof had caved in one bad winter, and I gritted my teeth. The neighborhood dogs had figured out a way to poke their muzzles through the gap in the warped kitchen door frame and wiggle inside. A few were always sneaking in. Some nights, I ignored their rumblings in the kitchen. But on evenings when my ma wasn't home, and there was nothing on TV, and Albert was holed up in our room, I would hide behind the stove with a basket of Zach's lacrosse balls. I'd see the nose poke in then the head. The dog would peek in, and though it could probably smell me, the scent of our stove must have been more compelling. I'd wait until the dogs were all the way in, then I'd jump out and whip the balls at their thick-furred hides. They'd turn and squeeze back through the frame, but by then I'd usually gotten some good wallops in.

I didn't like chasing the dogs away, and under the circumstances, they were even friendly. I hoped they understood it was just a matter of territory—that I couldn't let go of the idea I had a semi-normal house, however far-fetched.[27]

---

[26] Studying secondary characters in action is a good way to deepen comprehension.

[27] No doubt you and your students will see many craft moves in this passage: describing a setting using a list, using active verbs, and revealing a character through his thinking and actions. Although we may focus our lessons on individual craft moves, we must recognize that other craft moves will surface in student talk. Isn't that amazing? Every time students comment on craft moves they notice independently, I celebrate their growing understanding and reinforce their keen observation skills.

On Saturday we say good-bye to Dad. He makes me promise to look after the family, and then Joe ushers him away, reassuring us he's in good hands. I feel queasy just thinking about him in war zones. It sounded exciting at first. Now it seems like a stupid thing for him to have agreed to do.

Seeing my mum cry is tough. She's a strong woman and it takes a lot for her to break. I give her a big bear hug. She's short and plump and her head comes to my chest. She looks up at me, wiping the tears from her eyes.[28]

The time for taking the test was sliding away quickly. I was already behind. I needed to get started, or I wouldn't finish the test.

I set my pencil to work, but was it ever hard to concentrate! This was worse than being shoved into a cold pond when you're not expecting it, and landing face-first with a smack.

I was writing my answers fast and furious. I couldn't think about the answers, though. I'd studied for the test, but getting ready for a test takes more than just knowing the facts.

I need the warm-up in my mind—spending a minute picturing myself taking the test and doing good on it. And holding that picture in my thoughts till it's all I see in front of me.

I didn't have a minute, though. By the time I'd begun, I had less than twenty minutes to take a half-hour test.

The only warm-up in my mind was the thud of a headache starting as I tried to see the test questions clearly.

Then something changed.

Somewhere between filling in the blanks about the nervous system and respiration, the thud in my head turned to punching in my chest. At first, I thought it was my heart pounding past my ribs. But it was more than that—it was my intention. Then came the same voice I'd heard when Mama and I first set eyes on the papers that explained what my science lessons would be.

---

[28] Although the narrator takes only one direct action in this passage, it is in response to another character's action. I encourage students to look at actions a character takes independently, as well as those taken in response to other characters' actions, to deepen comprehension.

You can do this? You can do this?

The voice grew louder. My intention, simpler.

You can.

I raced through my answers, filling in the last question one second before Mrs. Elmer announced our time was up. The punching, pounding intention in me said, You did.

The Light in Hidden Places by Sharon Cameron

I go home and hang the curtains.

And at twenty minutes after six in the morning, I wander past the railroad station on my way home from work. Two men sit on the platform bench. They have caps pulled low on their heads, grease on their faces, lumpy bags that could be full of tools on their backs, and one holds a thermos with a handle. The one with the thermos is Max, and the other must be Siunek, and I'm not sure what kind of workers they're supposed to be. But whatever they are, they get off the bench and start moving in my direction.

I hold my coat closed tight to keep my hands from shaking, even though it isn't that cold, and walk at a leisurely pace toward Tatarska 3. And then I quicken my steps. There's a policeman coming down a side street, turning my way around the corner.

I don't dare look back. I'm supposed to distract a policeman. That's why I'm here. To keep the policeman's attention on me, and not the workers who aren't workers just a few steps behind.

But my brain is not coming up with the first way to do it.

And then I hear a voice say, "Stefania?"

I stop in my tracks. It's him. Officer Berdecki.

The Race of the Century by Neal Bascomb[29]

Very early on he recognized that he had a gift for running. He was never very good in a sprint, but if the game was to run around the block twice, he always won. In eighth grade, the high school coach came down to evaluate which kids were good at which sports. He threw out a football to see who threw or kicked it the farthest; a basketball to see who made a couple of jump shots. Then he told the kids to run to the grain elevator. Within a few hundred yards, Santee was all alone and knew he had the others whipped. He had run to the grain elevator and back and even taken a shower before the others returned.

What had started as fun—running to chase mice or the tractor—and had then become a way to escape from his father's clutches, was now a way to excel. Each race he won bolstered his pride. Over the next four years he scorched up the tracks throughout Kansas. He won two state mile championships and was targeted by college track recruiters from coast to coast.

The Sky Is Everywhere by Jandy Nelson

The Fontaine boys are like a litter of enormous puppies, rushing and swiping at each other, stumbling all around, a whirl of perpetual motion and violent affection.[30]

---

[29] Yes, using a list to describe actions crosses from fiction to nonfiction. I appreciate how Bascomb has chosen verbs to make his list visual and lively (e.g., *whipped, scorched*).

[30] I want to write like this.

Their Turn: Independent Practice

I spend a lot of time listening to authors discuss their work in podcasts and interviews.[31] When they talk about their processes, a common theme is revision, particularly deep cuts they make to first drafts. Those drafts often include long passages about characters that they eliminate as they reread. Sometimes, the entire character is eliminated!

The process of selection is directly related to intention. With the "down draft," most authors write quickly and excessively.[32] When they reread, though, they can see where zigzags and detours might confuse or frustrate a reader, and then they may streamline those spots because they know where they're going. But that process is invisible to us because we only see the final draft. So, we need to make it visible for students.

Years ago, my husband and I took our children to London on vacation. One morning, he took the kids to do laundry and encouraged me to visit the public library to see an exhibition of authors' first drafts. I was mesmerized. I came upon J. K. Rowling's writing and squinted through a glass case to read the paragraph she'd deleted from a Harry Potter book. I studied pages from Charlotte Bronte's first draft of *Jane Eyre*, written in gorgeous, symmetrical cursive, line after line, with only one phrase deleted. How did she draft with such precision?!

 TIP

Take a "Drone View" of Using a List

After noticing and imitating several micro mentor texts, pull back and study how authors often use a list as an organizing tool for an entire book. In their incredible story in verse, *Martin Rising*, writer Andrea Davis Pinkney and illustrator Brian Pinkney organize the last few months of Dr. Martin Luther King, Jr.'s life in stages or, for all intents and purposes, a list: first the prelude, then *daylight*, *darkness*, and *dawn*. Within each of those sections, they include a series of poems that tell the story of that stage in King's life.

---

[31] The Longreads Podcasts are brilliant… so many insights!

[32] Just get it "down" as you "draft." Everything goes in. You write as quickly as possible and ignore your inner censor, who may be telling you you're rambling. Momentum over analysis. This exercise often leads to finding a through line for the piece. If we always second-guess our sentences, we sputter and stop.

Of course, all the micro mentor texts in this book are final drafts. But we can imagine what came before. We can image what might have been cut. I ask students to pick a secondary character that is in a book they are reading—someone whom they know little about because the author does not provide details about him or her. I ask them to list what might have been—what they imagine, based on how that character figures into the overall story—and write a scene that reveals more about him or her. This is practice I always find engaging. With students, it is a home run for both deepening comprehension and strengthening writing.

Look closely at the titles of the three sections of Pinkney's *Martin Rising*. Each begins with a one-word title that starts with the letter *D*. Each one represents the light at a different time of day. That move is more powerful than choosing August, November, January, or first, second, last. The Pinkneys show their love of language by choosing those titles. They prove that a list can create imagery and each item on it can preview what is to come.

Chapter 3

Organizing Artfully: The Power of Three

"As a child, I was drawn to books with spunky heroines. They broadened my ideas of what was possible for me, as a girl. And they also taught me a little about how complicated human beings can be."

—Jesmyn Ward, two-time winner of the National Book Award

3a Tap the Power of Three Precise Details

3b Describe an Event With Three Details

3c Describe an Experience With Three Details

3d Define Actions in Nonfiction With Three Details

There is something magical about the number three. We think in past, present, and future. We write stories with a beginning, a middle, and an end. You're out on the third strike in baseball, or you marvel at the swish of a three-point shot in basketball. Hockey (and cricket) players strive for a hat trick, which is three goals in one game. You might have competed in a triathlon or cheered on a favorite horse in the Triple Crown.

We like to have choices, but not too many. Maybe that's why Goldilocks sat in three chairs, tasted three bowls of porridge, and considered three beds to sleep in. And it was three little pigs that had to deal with the wolf. Think of the last time you had your picture taken; the photographer may have counted *1-2-3*. The Olympics award three medals to athletes in each event: the gold, the silver, and the bronze. And did you know an octopus has three hearts? And a camel has three eyelids?

Yes, there is something magical about the number three. Perhaps that is why so many writers use three details to craft a description or three verbs to craft a character's moves. Once you start noticing the power of three, you will find examples of it in all you read.

3a Tap the Power of Three Precise Details

FIRST: NOTICE

Details help us to *see*, *feel*, and *understand* a moment captured in words, and we often rely on background knowledge to come up with them. We might use background knowledge of a grandmother, for example, to describe a scene that takes place at a family reunion. We all see characters and settings and situations a little differently, even when we read the same book. Our experiences are different, so the text is different. Precise details, however, provide the spark that ignites images as we read.

In this lesson, students practice imitating precise details in a nonfiction narrative by standing on the shoulders of writer Andrea Davis Pinkney. To learn a new skill, students must practice it many times over the course of a unit. I offer a series of practice opportunities that will help students become skilled at using precise details through repetition.

Martin Rising by Andrea Davis Pinkney	Details I Notice
Gwen has made fixin's for the soul: roast beef, candied yams, turnip greens.	• The phrase "fixin's for the soul" communicates the voice of the narrator—warm and friendly. • The apostrophe replaces a missing letter (in this case ' = g). • Because this is a book written in verse, the author has chosen to break the sentence into two parts. • Commas separate words in a series. • The three items are written in parallel structure: adjective noun. • The colon signals "here comes a list."

SECOND: IMITATE

Meaning matters. Voice matters. And punctuation and grammar matter. We focus our study first on the power of three precise details in the micro mentor text above, because if writing is always a struggle to get punctuation and grammar right, a student can lose interest. Studying micro mentor texts takes the sting out of punctuation and grammar because we study passages with curiosity and joy, while we create.

I begin with an image of my grandmother and write:

Grandma brought Easter dinner:

I think aloud. "I'm using the colon like Pinkney did. I know a colon means 'here comes a list.' Now I think about food my grandma would bring to dinner." I write:

Grandma brought Easter dinner: baked ham

I think aloud. "What else was on our dinner table? Oh, coleslaw. But I didn't like it," I tell students. "I want my list to help me remember good things." I add to my sentence:

Grandma brought Easter dinner: baked ham, fried chicken, mashed potatoes.

I reread my sentence out loud to students and add, "Now I think about the order of items on my list. Pulitzer Prize-winning writer and journalist Donald Murray told me that when you have three items in a list, the first one should be the second-most important, the one in the middle should be least important, and the last one should be the most important—because readers remember the last item most readily."[33]

I call this the 2-3-1 strategy, and I teach students to consider using it when designing arguments containing three pieces of evidence, when choosing historical or scientific points for "test writing," or when writing details containing three parts.

I reconsider my sentence above and say to students, "Baked ham is the star of Easter dinner at my house, so I will put it last. My Grandma Grace always brought fried chicken, so when I think of her, I think of chicken. That means I'll put potatoes in the middle because they are least important. You see, I loved mashed potatoes, but not the ones that Grandma picked up at a restaurant. I decide to add action to the start of the sentence, so I include how I felt when I saw the dinner arrive." I then share this completed imitation sentence:

My tummy rumbled when I watched Grandma unpack the Easter dinner: fried chicken, mashed potatoes, brown-sugar ham.[34]

YOUR TURN

I love both of the following micro mentor texts. You might select one that is a good fit for your students, or you could use all of them, spread out among several weeks of instruction. Repeated practice leads to retention.

---

[33] This sounds like newspaper-writer wisdom to me, but its roots may be deeper than that. The holy trinity, the three types of rhetorical appeals... Who knows?

[34] I added "brown-sugar" to create a bumpity-bump ending to my sentence. This revision is so much better! I want to keep writing, which is exactly the goal of this practice.

> **_Where the Crawdads Sing_ by Delia Owens**
>
> Reflecting sunlight, they [leaves] swirled and sailed and fluttered on the wind drafts.

> **_The Sky Is Everywhere_ by Jandy Nelson**
>
> I start to think about all the things I haven't said since Bailey died, all the words stowed deep in my heart, in our orange bedroom, all the words in the whole world that aren't said after someone dies because they are too sad, too enraged, too devastated, too guilty, to come out—all of them begin to course inside me like a lunatic river.
>
> *
>
> It's as if everything around us stops to see what's going to happen next—the trees lean in, birds hover, flowers hold their petals still.

3b Describe an Event With Three Details

FIRST: NOTICE

In the powerful book, *Martin Rising*, written by Andrea Davis Pinkney, there are many stellar examples of writer's craft.

In the following chart, what do you notice in the passage on the left? Try to name a few craft moves *before you read* "Details Student Pairs Might Notice" in the column I've filled in on the right.

 TIP

Pair Up Students to "Notice"

Allow students time to think and talk together in pairs about what they notice in the micro mentor text and then gather them to make a class list. This is a perfect opportunity to add information about grammar and sentence structure to bolster student understandings.

Martin Rising by Andrea Davis Pinkney	Details Student Pairs Might Notice
Struggling now to make sense of sudden lightning. *Daddy,* snatched, plucked, stolen—in a blink!— by the hand of a man filled with hate.	• The repeated "s" sound is pleasing to the ear (*struggling, sense, sudden*). • *Daddy* is in italics. The name is intimate. The italics soften the sound of the word, almost like a whisper. • The three verbs used to describe Martin Luther King, Jr.'s death have sharp sounds: *snatched, plucked, stolen.* • Commas separate the three verbs. • The exclamation point shows energy to amplify the phrase. That energy might be excitement, horror, fear, anger, or urgency, and all those emotions are expressed with the same punctuation, the exclamation point. • The phrase "in a blink!" is set off with dashes to show that it is an afterthought (but also for emphasis to show there was no time to help). • Because this is a book written in verse, the author has chosen to break the two sentences into parts and then separate the two sentences into stanzas. In poetry, stanzas operate like paragraphs. Consider where line breaks might have been made and how it changes the way this is read.

SECOND: IMITATE

I choose my daughter learning to ride a bike as a subject because it invites me to use multiple verbs. My imitation:

> *Hannah*
> *wobbled,*
> *teetered,*
> *pumped the pedals—and rode away!*

My first two verbs have similar meanings, just like the author's in the micro mentor text, and they describe perfectly my young daughter on her bike in front of our house. I ignore other details that come to mind as I write. I see the green of the trees around us that day, and I feel the warm June sun. Hannah's strawberry blonde hair is sticking out of her helmet and trailing behind her as she rides. The act of remembering not only brings me pleasure, but it also makes me want to write more. The act of converting memories into writing is energizing.

I look for an energetic ending phrase to complete the image. I imitate Pinkney by using a dash and exclamation point.

I reread my sentence and explain to students that I want to add more details at the start of my piece, in the spirit of the micro mentor text. I tell them, "I could say, 'On a June day.' But I want to be more precise: 'On Hannah's birthday we walked her bike to the end of our driveway.'" I play with ways to break that sentence to imitate Pinkney's form:

> *On Hannah's birthday*
> *we walked her bike*
> *to the end of the driveway.*
> *Hannah*
> *wobbled,*
> *teetered,*
> *pumped the pedals—and rode away!*

I tell students that my mentor Don Graves once told me (while he was writing a book of poetry) that line breaks often occur at a noun or a verb, so a strong word holds the reader's attention as she moves to the next line. At this point, I continue to work with my piece and invite students to get to work on their own. Once they have settled in, I leave my example projected on the screen in front of us and sit beside them individually to listen to them read what they are working on.

YOUR TURN

In another passage from *Martin Rising*, we see the power of three precise details to describe the subjects Martin Luther King, Jr. studied in school. What do you notice about word choice and order?

Martin Rising
by Andrea Davis Pinkney

He studied
oratory,
sociology,
theology,
and excelled.

Their Turn: Independent Practice

You might extend this imitation into many-verse poems. Ask students to list their favorite things (e.g., sports played, stories they've written, books they've read, towns they've lived in). Students will likely have lots of suggestions for categories. This could become a multi-verse poem, with each verse following the pattern in the micro mentor text above. One stanza might be about food and another about lullabies sung by a grandmother.

Once students have composed several stanzas, they must consider the order in which the stanzas should go. What is most important? Least? You might even create a book of class poems to share on Open House night.

But hold on a minute...

I am cautious about imitation, especially when teaching writing. I advocate notebook practice activities because I know they help writers think in creative ways about design and craft moves. But I balance those practice activities with frequent *freewriting* (e.g., The teacher reads a poem, and each writer chooses a personally meaningful line or phrase and writes quickly for several minutes.)[35] There are days when I have writers sketch from art postcards to study details. There are days when I ask students to practice dialogue or write freely about something that happened yesterday. In other words, I don't have them imitate every day. If I did, every student would soon grow bored of the practice.

I resist asking students to write the same thing in the same way as they move from notebook practice to best drafts. Any time we ask students to do that, we create a competition among them. Students are likely to assume someone else will do it better, so why even try? We must celebrate students' decision-making and problem-solving. And their creativity! Often the sentence that strays from the pattern is the most interesting one in the room. Be aware of that. I get nervous when I walk down the hall of a school and come upon a bulletin board where 30 snowmen all hold brooms in their right twig hands. (I'm sure you do, too.)

3c Describe an Experience With Three Details

FIRST: NOTICE

In the following chart, in the column on the left, is a short passage from *Boycott Blues*, written by Andrea Davis Pinkney. There are several writing craft moves in just 30 words!

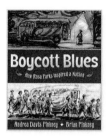

What do you notice? Try to name what you see *before you read* "Details I Notice" in the column I've filled in on the right.

Boycott Blues by Andrea Davis Pinkney	Details I Notice
Well, listen good. Because here it is. Steady. Slow. A story told with steps. With tired feet. With tired *bones*. This story walks. And walks. And walks. To the blues.	• The repetition (alliteration) of the "s" sound in *steady, slow, story, steps.* • The use of voice: *Well, listen good* implies a close relationship between reader and writer. • The intentional fragments: *with tired feet. With tired bones.* Students should consider why Andrea chose to write in fragments. What is the effect of these fragments on a reader? I hear steps that make the sentence walk to a beat. • The order of the list of how the story is told: *steps, feet, bones.* • Explore the metaphor of how a story can be told with tired bones.[35] • Consider the italics for *bones.* We know italics create emphasis; do all our students? Why is *bones* in italics? • Later in the passage, Pinkney uses straight repetition: *walks. And walks. And walks.* The periods make the reader slow down while reading the sentence.

---

[35] See Chapter 8: Using Literary Devices.

SECOND: IMITATE

There is power in taking an ordinary experience and making it more interesting. So, for a subject, I choose my seat on an airline.[36]

I write a list of observations:

> *Cold air blasts my left arm, my feet are jammed against the space in front of me, I hear the whine of engines warming up, there is a steady stream of passengers tugging roller bags, the flight attendant says, "Good morning!" to each passenger, other seated people are bent over screens, coffee cups in hand.*

I look at my list of observations. *Cold air* is an adjective-noun combination. I like that rhythm as a start. I try *Airline travelers*, but it sounds stuffy and formal. I delete it.

> *Weary passengers* (better!) *tug* (my favorite verb from my brainstorm list) *roller bags, cradle coffee mugs, and slump into their seats, fastening seatbelts.*

I reread and do not like the repeat of *seats* in the last phrase. So, I revise the sentence:

> *slump into worn seats, ready to fly.*

You likely noticed that I imitated a list of three things to describe an experience, using parallel structure. But my structure is different from the micro mentor text's. The passage inspired me to use a repeating pattern to define what it is like to travel by air. However, instead of a series of fragments, my phrases (verb-adjective-noun) are part of a complete sentence. This form felt most natural to me for this description. I like creating something beautiful (in my mind, at least) from the ordinary even if it leads me away from a direct imitation. When I see students do this in class, I recognize the variation and ask them why they chose it. We want students to be able to name the writing craft they use. Confident writers break patterns to craft original texts. This is what I hope micro mentor text study can do for all my students.

---

[36] Ever wonder how books get written by teachers who present at workshops, while still teaching? Fingers tapping, earplugs in, and laptop bouncing with every bit of turbulence. That's how.

YOUR TURN

Here are four passages in which authors use details to describe. Choose one that you feel is a good fit for your students and use it to study the power of this craft move, as I did in the last section.

Martin Rising by Andrea Davis Pinkney

Martin's memory
shines as
bright as
daffodils,
tulips,
orchids,
blooming in so many hearts.

The Red Pencil by Andrea Davis Pinkney

Muma and I talk easily about most things:
How best to stack kindling.
When sugarcane is ready to harvest.
Ways to peel potatoes.
But there is one thing Muma will not allow me
to address with her—school.

....

What they teach from those books
is useless to you, Amira.
We need you here, to milk our cows,
to pick okra and melons,
to rake.

Rhythm Ride by Andrea Davis Pinkney

Although laws had been passed that prevented segregation in public schools, in many states, black students and white students still attended separate schools. Black students still had shabby books, broken pencils, and rickety desks.

Infinity Ring: Curse of the Ancients by Matt de la Peña

She sees herself hurrying through flooding streets, out of breath, underneath a blistering twilight sky. Thick tornadoes ripping through neighborhoods in the distance. The bloodred sun hovering closer to Earth than seems possible, electrical surges shooting out from its core, making the swirling wind intolerably hot and sticky. Acid rain gushing down in slanted sheets. People leaning out of upper-story windows. All of them wide-eyed and screaming. Holding one another.[37]

---

[37] Matt has created a lovely variation of the pattern we are studying here. The first sentence has a list of three details to describe. This is followed by one sentence of description. The sentence that follows is again three details which describe, followed by four sentences that each hold one detail. I find this fascinating. The paragraph dips and whirls and breaks the expected pattern like the tornado he is describing. Gorgeous writing, as usual, from Matt de la Peña.

3d Define Actions in Nonfiction With Three Details

FIRST: NOTICE

Rhythm Ride by Andrea Davis Pinkney is a lively, engaging, historical account of the rise of Motown in Detroit, Michigan. The author's notes on studying the voice of a radio personality as she developed the text and the additional sources at the end of her book provide a comprehensive ride through the 1950s and 1960s. You will love it!

What craft moves do you notice in the following micro mentor text? Try to name a few *before you read* "Details I Notice" in the column I've filled in on the right.

Rhythm Ride by Andrea Davis Pinkney	Details I Notice
In parts of the South, if you were African American and wanted a burger and a Coke at a lunch counter, you would not be served at a "Whites Only" restaurant. And, chances are, if you were African American, some prejudiced person would try to get rid of you by spitting in your face or pouring hot coffee over your head.	• Verbs *do* heavy lifting when it comes to creating images for readers. Sentences sizzle with energy as you read because those verbs power the movie in your mind. *Spitting in your face* carries the force of anger, and *pouring hot coffee over your head* almost makes me duck. Andrea uses these phrases to demonstrate what she means by a person *trying to get rid of you.* • These two sentences provide an opportunity to study the use of commas. Teachers often ask how to teach the complexity of grammar and punctuation, and this offers one rich possibility. In the first sentence, a prepositional phrase provides context followed by the details of a scene, which is also set off from the engine of the sentence by a comma. (*In…, if…, you would not be served.*) With the second sentence the commas provide the natural pauses in voice: *And, chances are, if…,* followed by the heart of that sentence *some prejudiced person would…* • I study *both* the use of verbs and the use of commas in this passage.

SECOND: IMITATE

Memoirs and informational texts are both forms of nonfiction, and both are full of possibility for this imitation. I choose informational text and will try to write with the grace and precision of Andrea Davis Pinkney. My subject is Great East Lake in Acton, Maine. I look back at the micro mentor text and borrow the first phrase: *In parts of...*to begin writing my imitation. I am on my paddle board by 6:00, squinting into early sun. Can words capture the way the sunshine winks between the towering fir trees that line the shores in the narrows? I will try. I will reveal facts about this lake as I imitate the use of phrases and commas and vivid verbs in Pinkney's passage.

Here is my completed passage, followed by is my explanation of the decisions I made as a writer that I would model in front of students.

> *Down a quiet, winding road in central Maine, if you are looking to drop in your paddle board just after dawn, don't miss the silence and the expansiveness of Great East Lake. Originally called Lake Newichawannock by the Wabanaki Nations, the land surrounding this paradise was gobbled up by early settlers in the mid-19th century. And, chances are, if you remind your neighbors of this truth, they will insist on their right to land that was bequeathed to them across generations.*

I move between the book, *Newichawannock Reflections: Memories of Great East Lake* compiled by the Great East Lake Improvement Association in 1998 and revised in 2007, and the view out the windows of the house we purchased on its shores as I write. I use both a nonfiction resource and my own observations to compose.

I struggle. Sometimes I find it valuable to show students how I overcome a struggle. Even in composing my opening phrase, I revised several times. From *In central Maine*, which is a close imitation of the mentor text, to *Down a quiet, winding road in central Maine*, which brings readers into the beauty of the setting, not just its location. I am imitating Andrea Davis Pinkney, while also crafting my own voice and style.

I frame my next section around the phrase *if you are...* and then the writing takes a turn. When I write about the land's original stewards, the Newichawannock people, I find myself circling a new subject: Who owns the land? I use the verb *gobbled* to represent a ravenous hunger for this land and *bequeathed* because it means "passed on from one generation to the next." Pinkney has not only given me vision for writing about place, but phrases that led me to think deeply.

YOUR TURN

In the micro mentor text below, we see similar craft moves. As I did in the last section, first define what you see, and then attempt an imitation. You can then offer your students two lessons on comma usage and vivid verbs. Repetition cements learning.

Rhythm Ride by Andrea Davis Pinkney

Kids your same age suffered ugly violence. On March 2, 1955, a teenager named Claudette Colvin refused to give up her seat on a bus in Montgomery, Alabama, to a white woman after the driver demanded it. Claudette was dragged off the bus backward while being kicked by police and handcuffed on her way to the police station.

Their Turn: Independent Practice

I am mesmerized by Delia Owens's craft in *Where the Crawdads Sing*. From the minute I started reading it, I opened my notebook to collect passages of interesting writing craft. When you read a few of the examples I collected from that book, you will recognize immediately the power of three details to describe:

> *As she rounded a stand of tall grass, suddenly the ocean's face—gray, stern, and pulsing—frowned at her.*

Or the power of three verbs to define action:

> *Reflecting sunlight, they [leaves] swirled and sailed and fluttered on the wind drafts.*

Or the power of three comparisons to show growth in a young man over time:

> They had known Chase since he was born. Had watched his life ease from charming child to cute teen; star quarterback and town hot shot to working for his parents. Finally, handsome man wedding the prettiest girl.

This is a transition I hope all students make: from being led to see writer's craft by their teacher to discovering it on their own. And in fact, some of your students will probably see craft everywhere and willingly share it, week after week. Others, however, may not notice craft because they are so immersed in the story worlds created by authors. Both of those acts are important. Both represent engagement. Reading itself can be the greatest writing teacher. However, we do want all students to demonstrate this transition to independence, so I use two methods to support those who are not there yet.

SMALL GROUPS OR BOOK CLUBS

I sit with one book club during class when all the students are gathered in small groups to discuss their books. I bring my notebook where I have collected passages from reading the book they are reading. I share the micro mentor texts I have collected and lead a discussion of the craft moves we notice together.

Who contributes to this discussion? Who does not? My observations help me identify students who need additional instruction.

I repeat this practice with each book club. When I analyze my notes later, I can form a small group of students from all the book clubs who need additional modeling and practice. During our writing workshop time, I gather these students around me with a micro mentor text to reteach craft moves.

After this reteaching, I continue to observe students while they are discussing their books in book clubs, and I make note of students who are now able to contribute to a discussion of craft moves. I notice students who will benefit from additional instruction. I confer with them during our independent reading time.

READING CONFERENCES

Every day while students are reading, I meet with several of them one-on-one for reading conferences. These conferences might be centered on their stamina as readers, the challenges they seek, or how well they understand what they are reading.[38] It is also the perfect opportunity to reinforce how writing craft moves impact reading comprehension. For example, an author's descriptions of characters and events will help us create an image as we read, deepening our understanding of the moment.

Seated beside a student with a text he has chosen, I point out elements of writing craft we have studied on one page and ask the student to find an example on the next. After several turns, I ask the student to keep reading independently, but also to find an example he can add to his notebook page where he collects craft passages. I give the student a sticky note and ask him to mark the page and hand it to me as he leaves class. This way I can follow up with three to four students at a time until all have made the transfer from being led to see writer's craft to finding it without help.

[38] In *Book Love: Developing Depth, Stamina, and Passion in Adolescent Readers* (2012), I discuss various kinds of conferences and ways to manage a room of independent readers.

Chapter 4

Noticing What Dialogue Reveals

"Looking over a teacher's shoulder or crouching by a seven-year-old's desk, I lose myself in listening; at home, when I sit down to write, I remember and bring all those lands and lives to the page."

—Georgia Heard, *Writing Toward Home: Tales and Lessons to Find Your Way*

You know that moment when you hear a phrase in the voice of a loved one? I hear, "Go ahead, Pookah, keep your head down. I'll watch the ball." And I feel the quiet love in my father's voice: for his youngest daughter; for that one moment on a favorite golf course; for the startling beauty of June in Oregon. I see him again as I once did: his eyes on the pin, his hands resting on his hips, his silhouette framed by Mt. Hood in the distance and the towering Douglas firs that line each fairway. It's all there again. The whole scene unfolds with the memory of a few seconds of speech. We are bound to people we love in lots of ways, but one I want to think about in this chapter is patterns of language and repetition of phrases.[40]

Our memories and experiences are built on our senses. In this chapter, I focus on the *sound* of speech—in particular, the close study of how characters reveal who they are and what they believe by what they say and how they say it. You will notice in each micro mentor text that the author uses spoken words to provide details and evoke feelings. Skillful writers capture how speech distinguishes father from son, or one friend from another, or even what a character says from what he or she thinks. Sometimes we are given an inside view of characters' insecurities, hesitations, or worries, as well as their joys, wonders, and hopes through inner dialogue.

Dialogue leads to a fuller understanding of the people who drive a story, a poem, or a profile. The study of this craft move will have two major impacts on your literacy work:

1. Deepen comprehension as students infer information from the details supplied by an author.

2. Empower students to season their own work with the spirit of those they write about.

Dialogue has long legs. The more students study it, the more they will apply what they learn to analyze communication outside of books. They will hear everyday conversation differently after this study. They will become attentive to

---

[40] When I miss my father most, I see us back on the seventh tee at Glendoveer Golf Course or fishing side by side on the Wilson River. I've been writing in a notebook for most of my life, and when I stumble upon an entry that contains something my father said, it feels like he's close to me again. Capturing your experiences in a notebook is the greatest gift you can give yourself. I hope you'll discover that as you use yours for the practices I recommend in this book.

body language. They will recognize double-speak as they recognize intentional gaps between what adults say and what they do. They will look at text messages differently and perhaps incorporate them into their own writing after studying Coe Booth's novel *Caprice*. Buckle up for a ride through the art of conversation.

4a Reveal What Characters Say and How They Say It

FIRST: NOTICE

In the following chart, in the column on the left, is a short passage from *Land of the Cranes* by Aida Salazar. This is a novel in verse. This form appeals to many students who feel intimidated by pages and pages of words. Students respond to what author and National Ambassador for Young People's Literature, Jason Reynolds, calls the "breathing space" created by line breaks on a page of text (2017).

What do you notice in the passage? Try to name a few craft moves *before you read* "Details I Notice" in the column I've filled in on the right.

Land of the Cranes by Aida Salazar	Details I Notice
"Crane Poem Gallery" Before his nap today Papi asks to see my daily picture poem. I pull it out from my backpack and uncrumple the edges. *What marvel did you make today, Betita?* he asks in his Spanish-sounding English	• She calls him *Papi*. What names do students have for their fathers? • The first five lines in this verse give readers a setting for this moment. • He calls her daily picture poem a *marvel* before seeing or hearing it—gently inviting his daughter to share. That word reveals his kindness. • He calls his daughter Betita. Is this a nickname?

Land of the Cranes continued	Details I Notice
warm soft round words are air to me but so strange to others they call it an accent different, a little, from my own singsong East LA English.	• There are no quotation marks around what is said. • The speech is surrounded by other sensory details to bring the moment to life (*before his nap, backpack, uncrumple the edges*). • She describes his speech as "Spanish-sounding English," then expands to define that as "warm soft round words." • Why run three adjectives together: *warm soft round*? There is more than one plausible answer.[41] I think it might be because the sound of his speech feels warm and soft and round all at once. Or maybe it is because if there were commas between the adjectives the reader might think some of the words are warm, some are soft, and some are round. • This metaphor, *words are air to me*, can mean many things. Does the character mean "necessary"? Light? All around her? • Singsong East L.A. English is familiar to students in California, I imagine, but unfamiliar to me. I want to hear it. The study of this passage is an opportunity to celebrate the differences in our multiracial society. We learn colloquialisms from our families and neighborhoods, from our friends and from music, books, television shows, etc. • Because this is a novel in verse, I notice the phrasing and the shape of this passage as a poem. I will imitate that.

[41] You've heard me say, "You can't do this wrong! Aida Salazar is not here, so we can make guesses as to what she is communicating by organizing her writing like this." It helps students share their observations with greater confidence.

SECOND: IMITATE

Imitating verse is more difficult for me than imitating prose, which is why I chose to attempt it. I like to challenge myself to do what I think I cannot.[42] And I know that the only way I will gain confidence in imitating verse is to try it and try it again. I move to my notebook to experiment.

First, I copy the passage and think about each word as I write it. (Copying the words of another writer helps me tune into them, while freeing my mind to think about my own words at the same time.) I consider who I could write about and make a mental list of possibilities, crossing off those I just don't want to write about today.

I can't seem to decide on a subject, so I look at the passage again and notice that it begins with the setting. I look up at my front door and write a moment that happened there—it is a moment I want to hold onto. I write:

> We are crowded
> by the front door
> to say goodbye. Cam says,
> Give Grandma a hug, and my
> almost-four-year-old Maisie
> climbs on to my feet
> and then wraps her legs and arms
> around me like a tiny monkey.
> She clings—

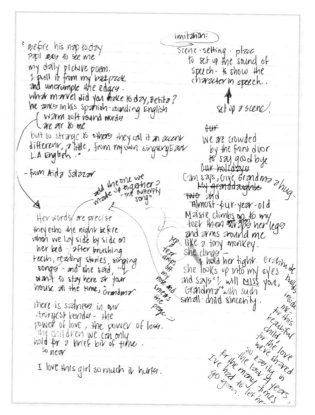

---

[42] It is important to share this part of the writing process with our students: how we struggle, what we learn when we challenge ourselves, how we overcome hurdles as writers. We are not supposed to be perfect models of writing, but rather, imperfect models of how writers work to make words match their intentions.

I stop here and look back at Salazar's passage, realizing that I have detailed Maisie's actions but not her words. I skip a line and write:

> *She looks into my eyes*
> *and says, I will MISS you, Grandma*
> *with such small-child sincerity*

As I write those lines, I hear Maisie beside me; I hear her emphasis on "MISS," which prompts me to go back and add to the moment:

> *She clings—*
> *I hold her tight.*
> *Gratitude builds inside me—*
> *for this beautiful child,*
> *for the love we've shared so easily*
> *in the last four years*
> *for the many times*
> *I've had to let her go*
> *again.*

 TIP

Share Your Joy!
Writing brings the wonder of ordinary days to the page. Show the snow at the window as you frost cookies beside two toddlers. Write the late afternoon quiet as you rake leaves. Create young writers who notice beauty, who delight in telling stories, who live wide awake to possibility.

In my notebook on page 81, you'll see what I add after this.[43] I hope you'll give me the grace to write badly in this first draft. If I work to shape this moment, the writing will improve. Sometimes I do that with students, and sometimes I just show them where a piece of writing starts.

I want to keep writing and revising, which is the goal of these imitations. They are invitations to do more. They might lead a young writer to develop an entire story or essay or poem from this start with Salazar. Or that writer's small bit of writing might stay nestled in the notebook for months, waiting to sprout at another time.
I decide to take this notebook work into my classroom and talk about revisions with students.

---

[43] You see those smeared words in my notebook? They are from a tear that dropped off my nose. Robert Frost famously said, "No tears in the writer, no tears in the reader. No surprise in the writer, no surprise in the reader." Writing goes straight to our hearts. Even in class sometimes.

I say, "We study how authors use dialogue to expand a scene and to give life to the characters there. When imitating a novel in verse, there are additional crafting decisions to make.

I must decide where to break lines. Line breaks convey meaning: They are directions to a reader on how to listen to the passage or how to read it aloud. I play with phrases: Should I indent some of them? What does it mean if I do? What does it mean in Salazar's model?"

As I write and think aloud with students, I model the decision-making that all writers do to align their words to the experience they are trying to create. This is your work as you lead your students through the imitation process.

YOUR TURN

The four passages below reveal characters by showing what is said and how it is said. Pick one or more to study with students.

Land of the Cranes by Aida Salazar

He kisses his pride right onto
my cheek with an extra-loving push
that makes my head wobble.
You sign just like an artist, mi Plumita.
    I thought maybe like a poet, Papi, I say
    because Ms. Martinez just taught us about
    Juan Felipe Herrera, the poet of the nation
    who is a crane like us.
Yes, like a poet too, amor.

Illegal by Francisco X. Stork

Gustaf continued, his voice softer, "I can't tell you what to do, but I've lived long enough to know that sometimes we find where we belong from the places we don't."

Illegal by Francisco X. Stork

"Let me go ahead and say it," Sandy said, removing her hand from mine and balling it into a fist. "This is ridiculous! This is...I don't even know what to call it. This is... unbelievable!"[44]

Caprice by Coe Booth[45]

I hope you are all excited to get started, the art teacher, Olivia, says to everyone. Her eyes are wide and there's a singsong in her voice.

Salazar does not use quotation marks around spoken words. I do not know why, so I make a guess. Sometimes when we remember conversations we've had, we don't know the exact words said, but only how it made us feel. Salazar's character may be repeating the conversation to show us her Papi's gentleness, but without using quotation marks because she can't remember his exact words. Or perhaps it is because this is a novel in verse and that genre operates with more fluid conventions, open to how the writer wants the words to appear on the page. I would love to ask her. Rather than treat conventions as right or wrong, consider an author's intentions with students. Approach unconventional moves with curiosity.

We will now move from the study of one character's speech to conversations between characters. This increases the complexity of students' thinking about dialogue because a conversation develops as both parties contribute thinking. What I say changes when I'm speaking to someone versus when that person

---

[44] Sandy's hesitation is represented here by an ellipsis, which increases tension because we all know what it feels like to search for the right words when we're frustrated. Her speech invites students to study what and how people speak when angry. The writer wonders, "How can I represent Sandy's frustration? How can I show the pauses as she tries to collect herself between phrases?" In this case, the writer chose an ellipsis.

[45] In this novel, the action occurs primarily in the final days of summer. The main character, Caprice, has spent the summer at a boarding school, where she has been accepted as a full-time student. As she wrestles with her decision to return to the school, we learn about her past through flashbacks to a sexual assault that she has never shared with anyone. The book is multi-genre; Caprice's struggle is conveyed through her poems, text messages, and her narration. Students will love Caprice. My eighth and ninth graders used to stand in line at my classroom door and wait for a student to return the author's earlier novel Tyrell. I would add both to your library.

responds to my thinking with his own.[46] The examples in the next section are rich with possibility and invite students to use dialogue between characters in their narratives, both in fiction and memoirs.

4b Capture Conversations Between and Within Characters

FIRST: NOTICE

For this study, we return to the gorgeous writing in *King and the Dragonflies* by Kacen Callender.

What do you notice in the passage? Try to name a few craft moves *before you read* "Details I Notice" in the column I've filled in on the right. In this study we pay attention to what is said and *how* it is said, especially as two characters navigate the awkwardness of adolescence.

King and the Dragonflies by Kacen Callender	Details I Notice
My leg starts to bounce up and down. I don't know why that makes me so angry—that she'd let Sandy read whatever's in her notebook, but not me. Does she think she's better friends with Sandy? It's not like I should care. Khalid used to tell me that guys aren't supposed to care about that kind of thing, so I pretend I don't. "What's it about?" I ask her.	• This shows the paragraphing that represents a shift in who is speaking in dialogue. It is important to emphasize that with students because it is a skill many of them struggle to master. • Many sections begin with "I say" or "She says" at first, but then the author discontinues using those attributions. Once the pattern is established, authors often drop the attributions since they interrupt the natural flow of conversation that a reader hears.

---

[46] Imagine when I lectured my son, who had been caught speeding. He sat silently and let me rant. When he responded, the conversation, both in tone and in the words spoken, shifted.

She starts to blink a whole lot. "It's just a story," she says.

"About what?"

She takes a deep breath. "About a girl who gets a crush on a boy but doesn't know how to tell him."

Hearing that alone makes my stomach twist. Jasmine still isn't looking at me, and I start to get the feeling—a bad, bad feeling—that she might be writing about me. Heat starts to grow from the pit of my stomach like a seed was planted there, and roots become all tangled in my chest and a stalk goes up my throat, and the flower that blooms from my mouth is a simple, "Ew."

Details I Notice

- So much is communicated in *she starts to blink a whole lot.* I would ask students to tell me what they think that means—what Jasmine might be feeling. This is a show, don't tell moment in a text worth looking at closely.

- The dash interrupts the text to define the feeling. I have students act out what this sounds like, almost like the author is sharing a secret. Students might whisper, for example.

- The description of heat is brilliant: The movement from pit to seed to roots to stalk to flower. This is an extended metaphor. Look at this with students and imitate its power with a different comparison.[47]

SECOND: IMITATE

Every imitation begins with the same challenge: how to start writing. I show them two ways I might start using ideas from two passages of Callender's writing—the one above and the one on page 88.

1. **Drop into the middle of a moment when you feel strongly. Start with a piece of dialogue.** My daughter yells from the other room, "Mom, will you take Julius out? I took him last time." I feel a jolt of annoyance—when I'm writing here in my office my family treats it like I'm shopping or wasting time. Writing is serious WORK.

---

[47] Here's my attempt. What if I use the growing feeling of doom when on a sled? *Fear builds as my father drops my sled at the top of the hill. My fear is a small pebble. We gain speed, and the pebble grows into a rock. I'm not sure about this. We hit a bump, and I feel the sled leave the snow—nothing but air beneath us. I scream. The boulder in my stomach makes me queasy. I hold tight to my father's coat as we coast to a stop and that boulder collapses into gravel. We stop. I start breathing again, swallowing a rusty aftertaste where I bit my tongue.*

2. **Imagine what you would say to someone you can't speak to.** I think, who have I lost? What would I want to ask? I think of Grandma Grace, my father's mother. My mind lights up. I like this idea. Students often think of pets, friends, homes they used to live in.

Of these two choices, I know I feel the most energy for writing about my grandma.[48] To look for a way to start, I go to another passage by Callender. In this passage, which is on the next page, Callender writes: "I want to ask Khalid—I want to ask him, 'Why did you choose—'"

I have many questions for my grandma, but first I want to introduce her to you. I'm ready to write.[49]

> *Grandma Grace died at 90, so you'd t hink I had plenty of time to ask her all I wanted to know about her life. I didn't. I moved away to college to teach in California, and when I returned to Oregon, I got married and started a family. I saw her straight-backed profile at gatherings on holidays, but our conversations rarely moved beyond pleasantries.*
>
> *There was one night, though, when she told my mom, my dad, and me a story from decades before. I wish I could go back and hear more. I want to ask her, "How did you put my dad on that train? He was going to travel alone from Minnesota to Oregon as a three-year-old, you told me. Weren't you afraid? You said you stayed up all night stroking his cheek, knowing how desperately you would miss him, but you never mentioned if sending him on a train for several days alone was haunting you as well. What am I missing here?"*

---

[48] This energy for writing is an emotional cue that I am ready to write. Kelly Myers wrote in *College Composition and Communication*, "Students should become familiar with emotional as well as intellectual cues that tell them they are ready to write, ready to stop, and ready to do a number of things in between."

[49] Did this glimpse of my process help you? Might your process help the young writers in your classroom? We create connections to our stories and the people we care about in writing, but we also show the way. That's powerful modeling, a bridge for writers who need a nudge.

And if she were still in that living room on Francis Street instead of buried six feet below the sunshine, she might look at me with wonder and say, "I'm glad you asked." Because too often the elderly people in our families sit off to the side at holidays and we don't listen to them. We miss our chances.

YOUR TURN

Below are three conversations from great books. Share two or more with students and compare the texts.

King and the Dragonflies by Kacen Callender

I want to ask Khalid—I want to ask him, "Why did you choose a dragonfly? Why not something cooler, like a lion or a panther or a wolf?" And if he were still in the body that's now buried in the ground over in the Richardson cemetery, he might hit me upside the head with his crooked grin and say, "Let me alone. I can choose to be whatever I want." And I wouldn't be able to argue, because I know he'd be exactly right about that.

Infinity Ring: Curse of the Ancients by Matt de la Peña

Dak tapped Sera on the arm and motioned toward Riq. "I liked it better when we hated this guy."

"We never hated him," Sera said.

"Speak for yourself."

"Believe me," Riq said. "The feeling was mutual."

"Maybe we should turn back the clock," Dak said. He elbowed Sera and gave her a big, goofy smile. "Get it? Turn back the clock?" He pointed at the Infinity Ring tucked safely back inside the satchel hanging from her belt.

"You truly are a child," Riq said.

"And you're a clown."

"Stop," Sera said. "Please. I need to think. If there are no conquistadores, like Dak said, maybe we really are in the wrong time. Because we're definitely in the correct geographical area."

"You're early." It's Bree, the girl with the light blue hair, and she's standing right over me.

I close my notebook fast. "Oh, I didn't hear you."

"I'm like a cat," she says laughing. "I sneak up on you!" She sits down next to me. "Is that whole book filled with poems?"

"Um, yeah, kinda. They're not really poems. Just like, thoughts, that—"

She holds her hand up to stop me from talking. "We have a rule around here, We never put our writing down. The world is hard enough for writers. We don't need to beat ourselves up, too."

I smile. I like that.

4c Capture the Dialogue of Text Messages

FIRST: NOTICE

Perhaps you've noticed how much we're all texting these days. While working on this chapter today, I've had three threads going with friends. I remember when students first started using acronyms (such as *LOL*) to replace speech, and many parents and teachers felt that it would ruin written language. I think we can all appreciate the ease and convenience of messaging now. Has it ruined written language? Not at all. It has enhanced it. My mom is in a different time zone, for example, and texting allows us to initiate a conversation regardless of the time of day. We use emojis to shortcut our feelings and thoughts. We search for the right GIFs to punctuate our family text threads.

It is worth studying text conversations because students are initiating and participating in them regularly. Authors such as Coe Booth are weaving those conversations into novels. Studying the examples that follow will show you how differently texts are punctuated.

We don't expect text messages to carry all the punctuation of a professional book like this one. In fact, my current students complain that I'm the only one they know who uses capitals and proper punctuation when I text. It is also true that we learn to change registers naturally in speech depending on whom we are talking to. Now we've added an additional medium where the rules are still being created by the users! This can feel confusing, but I think it helps us all think more deeply about conversation itself. Its form changes based on the message and the recipient of the message.

Our students change registers with ease—they speak differently to parents or teachers in person and in a text message than they do to their friends or when commenting anonymously on a post. Their language communicates the closeness of the relationship and often the age of the recipient.

In the micro mentor text that follows, *Caprice* by Coe Booth, the narrator, Caprice, messages one of her friends. Ask your students to identify what they notice about the conversation. What do they infer based on what they read?

Caprice by Coe Booth	Details I Notice

"I'm not restless," I say. It's just hard sitting still, bored. Especially since Mom is on the couch and she and Lana are talking, completely ignoring me. They're best friends like me and Nicole, and they have a lot to catch up on, too.

> **Sorry I didn't say goodbye**

Five seconds later she texts back.

> where were you after the party you vanished

> **I was with terra. how's kimberly? having fun in toronto?**

> yeah. my little brother wants to marry her! he's 7!!!

> **haha.**

> will i ever see you again you coming back next summer

It takes me a minute to decide if I should do this, but I decide to tell her about Dr. Suzanne's offer. Half a second later I get a

>  yay!!!

- Text messages are shortcuts. This is what we expect, so it is no wonder that the character begins straight to the point. This is also indicative of characters who know each other well.

- The author adds thoughts of the character to separate important moments in this text thread.

- The time between texts sent and the reply can say a lot. We've all waited for an answer, checking and rechecking. Especially after an apology! Five seconds might feel like 60.

- A run of questions is written in fragments.

- *haha* is a common acknowledgment, but it is quickly being replaced by emojis and GIFs. You might create a list of students' favorites of both. How has this flexibility changed text communication?

- The time between texts can lead one person to change what he or she was going to say, as happens here in the last line.

SECOND: IMITATE

Yikes, this looks hard! I'm going to study the model carefully before I draft. I like how the author added thoughts of the character in between the texts. I also like how authentic the string appears: the way text messages appear on my phone. I imitate both of those moves.

I get a text from my friend, Yukari. I always read hers, unlike some messages, immediately.

> *What time do you land at PDX?*
>
> *Not until 4. Stuck in Detroit.*
>
> *Bummers.*

This is one of Yukari's favorite expressions, and it makes me smile. I can't wait to see her.

> *Are you going straight to your mom's?*
>
> *Yep.*
>
> *Want to grab dinner with us? Mom would love to see you.*
>
> *I think she likes you better than me—no, I know she does.*
>
> *Ha. I'll text you.*
>
> *Safe travels.*

We've been best friends for 47 years,[50] so our texts sound a lot like our in-person conversation. Notice that even though we're best friends, and we text a lot, we both use punctuation, which reveals a little about who we are. Fragments are common (*Stuck in Detroit*) and so are last-minute plans. I ask students what they infer from this exchange.

I encourage students to play with this form, believing fully that they will bring their understanding of how text messages work to their writing. They could choose two characters in one of the micro mentor texts from this book or from a novel they are currently reading. Imagine an argument between them— or a request that one has for the other. I brainstorm with my students possible

---

[50] Yes, I said it, 47 years. That makes me twice as old as some of you reading this. I hope we can still be friends, though, because then I can show you our photos from high school.

situations (e.g., arguing over X, requesting Y) to give them ideas, and I would encourage each of them to work with a partner.

YOUR TURN

Select a passage below that you feel is a good fit for your students and use it to demonstrate the dialogue of text messages, as I did in the last section.

Caprice by Coe Booth

A minute later I get another text, this time from Nicole.

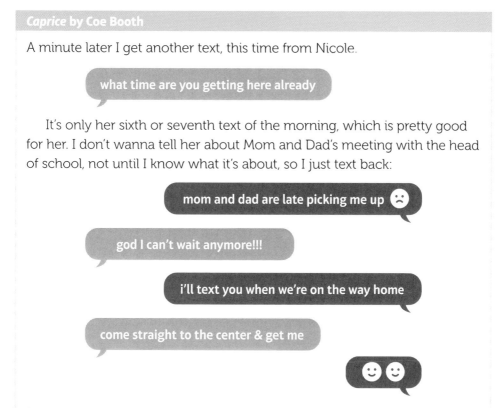

> what time are you getting here already

It's only her sixth or seventh text of the morning, which is pretty good for her. I don't wanna tell her about Mom and Dad's meeting with the head of school, not until I know what it's about, so I just text back:

> mom and dad are late picking me up 😟

> god I can't wait anymore!!!

> i'll text you when we're on the way home

> come straight to the center & get me

> 😊 😊

Seven weeks away hasn't been easy—not for either of us. I miss her so bad, and I know she misses me, too. Since I've been here, me and her texted all the time, but there's hardly been time for anything else. I hadn't actually heard Nicole's voice since my first week here.

Terra takes her blanket and sheets off her bed. "I was hoping our parents would get to meet each other," she says. "But my mum only left D.C. about two hours ago."

I'm in my bedroom, surrounded by study reinforcements (junk food), with music cranked up to a volume that would antagonize my mother but not the neighbors. Maha texts me while I'm doing a character profile of Mr. Knightley for my English homework.

> **Maha:**
> Jasmine got caught cyber-stalking Jasper so Paul dumped her & Jasmine's gone all "I have an eating disorder my world has ended" but we know it's just an act because we busted her gorging on veg toast and claiming she hasn't eaten in days.

It's random, frivolous, and gossipy but the familiarity of that voice sends a pang through me.

We send each other texts back and forth. Maha makes me ache with a longing to return to Auburn Grove Girls High, which was a kaleidoscope of cultures and ethnicities. Somewhere where I'm not the ethnic supporting character.

> **Maha:**
> Relax. You'll fit in soon.

> **Me:**
> I'm NOT using that whitening cream.

> **Maha:**
> Calm down. Nothing wrong with cosmetically changing your race to fit in.

> **Me:**
> You worry me.

> **Maha:**
> Nina just brought back a batch from India & swears by it but Pretti tried it and burned her skin. 😞

> **Me:**
> OMG. Where?

> **Maha:**
> Left butt cheek. She thought it best to try it in an inconspicuous spot first.

> **Me:**
> You worry me.

> **Maha:**
> Chillax. You moved suburbs not countries.

Their Turn: Independent Practice

One of my favorite invitations to students during a study of story is to be a "dialogue catcher." I ask them to pay attention to the things people say and how they say them by eavesdropping during lunch or while walking to the library or the playing field. Listen on the school bus. See what you notice about how people talk and the inferences you make as you listen.[51] When students record these in notebooks, they catch hold of them for future use in their own writing.

This is also a great time to revisit our collecting sheets, described in Chapter 1. Students can be led to catch dialogue in the books they are reading. Add "dialogue" to one of the sections for students to collect language they like. Share dialogue that you see in a book you are reading that you think is skillful. We can and must make the connection between what we read and how we write for our students. Every book is a great writing teacher, after all.

 TIP

Add Collaborative Writing to Your Instructional Playbook

Writing Next, a 2007 report from the Carnegie Corporation (available at pennykittle.net), contained 11 effective teaching strategies for adolescents, including collaborative writing—planning, drafting, revising, and editing together. When I first read the report, I was struck by collaborative writing because I simply wasn't using it enough. I have used it each year since the report was released. Definitely add it to your instructional playbook!

---

[51] Students *love* this assignment. Sometimes their parents and siblings don't, however. Ha!

Chapter 5

Developing Scenes

"Begin with the first thing that occurs to you, and keep adding to it, trusting your memory to reveal what is important. Sometimes the most trivial moments end up being the crucial ones in a life. So trust that, if you remember it, it is necessary to set it down."

—Esmeralda Santiago, from
The Autobiographer's Handbook

You've seen an accordion player, I'm sure. She presses keys for chords and then expands and contracts the folded bellows at the center to create variation in sound.[52] Stories are built with this same sense of contraction and expansion, only with scenes.

I once had our music director come to my class to play an accordion to make that connection clear to my students. We expand moments in time (stretch the bellows apart) that are important in developing our ideas, and then we contract whole days or even years (push the bellows together) to speed past them because they're not all that important. An hour-long scene might develop over a page and a half, for example, followed by five years in a sentence. This chapter focuses on what teacher, writer, musician, and dear friend Barry Lane calls "Exploding a Moment."[53] When a writer slows down time, detailing what is seen and heard so the reader experiences every sensation, that is exploding a moment.

Imagine the possibilities in story. I want to write about my father: I see us side by side on the Wilson River with fishing lines in the water, waiting for steelhead. Silent. I see us riding in one of his old American cars, his arm out the open window, his deep blue eyes hidden behind dark glasses. There he is in the dining room, doing a shuffle dance to the music of Roger Miller, his beautiful bass voice warm and relaxed in sync with Miller's voice. I see him in his recliner, leaning back, watching

---

[52] If you've never seen an accordion player—or have and want to see one again—I recommend "Great Street Music in London. Pretty Talented Accordion Player" on YouTube.

[53] Wait! Stop. If you search the Internet for "Exploding a Moment," a long list of links will appear. Don't jump to Teachers Pay Teachers, where people have taken Barry's work and created worksheets. You don't need those. I think children could live their lives quite happily without ever being given another worksheet. Instead, watch Barry explain this craft move in a four-minute YouTube video called "Explode a Moment with Barry Lane." You won't be sorry.

the television. I stop. That memory is dancing too closely to memories of his drinking years. Scratch that. I want to write something beautiful, a tribute to his many gifts. (What power lies in the hands of the storyteller. I *choose* what to tell, and how you, the reader, will understand my father.)

I select a moment from the thousands of moments my father and I spent together: the same task our students face when they choose a big subject from their life to write about, from the second grader writing about his skill with magic tricks to the twelfth grader writing about a beloved grandparent whom he recently lost.[54] We all face the same challenges: what to include, what to leave out. As teachers we must ask ourselves: How will I face these challenges with students? Can I show them how to unravel the complexity of writing without resorting to formulas? The writing process leads to discovery and creation. As we write, we find ideas. As we imagine one scene, another appears. Too much planning, too many restrictions, and the writer's focus shifts from creating to sticking to a plan. Too often we teach writing as organized, predictable thought. Writers know that's foolish; ideas take detours, and following them often leads to better writing.

START WITH ONE SCENE—NOT THE WHOLE STORY

I explain to students, a scene is just one moment in time. So I encourage them to start there. Many students think all details in a story matter. I once sat beside a fifth grader who wanted to share a trip that included the Space Mountain ride at Walt Disney World. He wrote, "We got up and brushed our teeth. Then we got in the car and drove to the airport. Then we had a pretzel. Then we flew on a plane..." By the time the student wrote his way to Space Mountain, a page and a half later, his interest in the topic had waned. The ride was reduced to one more item in a list of activities: "I rode on Space Mountain.[55] It was fun." It took the young writer a great deal of work to write about the airport and the pretzel, so cutting those parts would likely discourage him.

---

[54] Nancie Atwell called large, important subjects *territories*. I love that distinction: larger than a state, they are expansive and rich with possibility. We all have them. A few of mine are teaching, tennis, cancer, guitar, and 37 years of marriage to the greatest man I know. What are yours?

[55] If we look only at this writing, we might feel discouraged. It isn't that he doesn't know how to write well; the topic is so large that every detail feels important to him. Remember that studying student writing helps us understand what students need. As I look at his draft I think, *what does this writer need to understand about story?* I use the answer to focus a mini-lesson or small-group work the next day.

It would discourage any of us. That's why I tell students, "Let's just imagine one scene, one moment in time, and slow it down. Which scene out of all that happened on that trip do you want to help readers experience with you?"

I might go on to say, "Write one scene from your life using as many vivid, sensory details as you can. Write in a voice that is comfortable for you, like the one you would use with a best friend when you tell the story. Include dialogue so that your scene does not read like a silent movie. As you write this scene, you'll see how those details bring the experience to life."

I often see things so clearly in my memory, but I can't make words cooperate. I liken it to sketching. I look out my window and want to capture the pink roses that are filled with blooms this afternoon. As I sketch, I am frustrated by how hard it is to accurately represent the varied tones of color, the way buds rise from the stem, the way petals layer onto one another. But the more I work, the more I realize that my approximations are beautiful on their own. When you look in my notebook, the flowers won't be nearby, so you won't be able to compare them to what I have drawn. You'll (hopefully) just enjoy my sketch. When you read my piece about my father, you won't be standing on the golf course beside me, so any details I forget to mention won't feel forgotten to you. You'll enjoy this glimpse into our time together and what I have to say about it. Trust yourself to write well enough to create an experience for readers. Trusting yourself as a writer is an important quality to model for your students.

GO WHERE THE SCENES LEAD

Each of those moments with Dad can be a scene, and from them I might find a theme by thinking about them deeply. Will I focus on my father's natural ability as a teacher? Then I'll select lessons on the water, in the backyard with a fly rod, or on the golf course. Do I want to write about his silliness? That leads me to dancing on the course when he sunk a putt or calling me Chowderhead with a deep chuckle when I wouldn't take the fishing rod because the size of the Steelhead scared me. I would have to include that scene of him dancing a shuffle to "You Can't Roller Skate in a Buffalo Herd" or one of his ridiculous jokes. The act of imagining the stories I haven't written yet is engaging. I resist planning too far ahead, and instead write one scene and see what the writing of it leads me to think about next.

I write to discover what I have to say. I need freedom. Writing one scene might lead me to a perfect next moment in my piece that I had forgotten. I sit up straighter and celebrate the discovery. I think of scenes as puzzle pieces, and I can move them freely because I am still working to see the whole picture. This is art—and making it is gratifying, sustaining, and completely engaging.

We can teach that to writers. We should, in fact. After all, we want students to be flexible thinkers who craft their experiences into art. We want sustained engagement with writing; we want deep thinking. We want students to imagine possibilities. We don't want students who need our outline to write about snakes. We want their vision structured into a logical movement of thought. Helping them establish that vision develops their skill and confidence.

Lucky for us, novels are filled with scenes. We have hundreds of mentor texts at our fingertips. Let's begin with one from the incredible three-narrator story *Refugee* by Alan Gratz.

5 Use Scenes as Building Blocks in Stories

FIRST: NOTICE

In the chart on the next page, in the column on the left, is a short passage from *Refugee* by Alan Gratz. It captures a scene in a novel that crosses time and experience. I hope you have it in your library.

What do you notice in the passage? Try to name a few craft moves *before you read* "Details I Notice" in the column I've filled in on the right. In fact, I'm guessing you will find details I didn't notice. There is just so much rich writing craft in this passage.

Refugee by Alan Gratz	Details I Notice

It was like they were invisible.

Josef and his sister followed their mother through the crowd at the Lehrter Bahnhof, Berlin's main railway station. Josef and Ruth each carried a suitcase, and their mother carried two more—one for herself, and one for Josef's father. No porters rushed to help them with their bags. No station agents stopped to ask if they needed help finding their train. The bright yellow Star of David armbands the Landaus wore were like magical talismans that made them disappear. Yet no one bumped into them, Josef noticed. All the station attendants and other passengers gave them a wide berth, flowing around them like water around a stone.

The people chose not to see them.

On the train, Josef and his family sat in a compartment labeled J, for Jew, so no "real" Germans would sit there by accident. They were headed for Hamburg, on the north coast, where his father would meet them to board their ship. The day they had gotten Papa's telegram, Josef's mother booked tickets for all four of them to the only place that would take them: an island half a world away called Cuba.

Ever since the Nazis had taken over six years ago, Jews were fleeing Germany. By now, May of 1939, most countries had stopped admitting Jewish refugees, or had lots of official applications you had to fill out and file and pay for before they would let you in. Josef and his family hoped to one day make it to America, but you couldn't just sail into New York Harbor.

- The claim in the first sentence makes me curious. How were they invisible?

- The spelling of Josef indicates Germany to me, and there are more clues in the title of the train station and the name of the city, Berlin. More details will make this setting clear as we keep reading.

- Notice the repetition of "No" to show what was unusual in this moment. "No porters rushed..."; "No station agents stopped..."; "...no one bumped into them..."

- The simile creates an image of movement and flow that stays with me: *flowing around them like water around a stone.*

- The timeline of how they ended up in this train station is detailed after we experience the moment in the station. We see the characters in the setting first, and perhaps, have sympathy for them. Then we hear about their journey. The slowing down time as they walk in the station and onto the train engages us in storytelling. The list of events that follows is background, which we wouldn't pay attention to without first engaging with the characters in their story.

- The list of information is followed by dialogue ("I'm hot," Ruthie said...) to reengage readers in this moment.

Refugee continued	Details I Notice
The United States only let in a certain number of Jews every year, so Josef's family planned to live in Cuba while they waited. "I'm hot," Ruthie said, pulling at her coat. "No, no," her mother said. "You must leave your coat on and never go anywhere without it, do you understand? Not until we reach Cuba." "I don't want to go to Cuba," Ruth whined as the train got under way. Mama pulled Ruth into her lap. "I know, dear. But we have to go so all of us will be safe. It will be an adventure."	• I think back over this scene and notice all the things the author chose not to include. We don't see them packing up things and leaving precious books, heirlooms, or clothing behind. We don't see their goodbyes to friends or shopkeepers. We don't see a longing glance as they leave their home and town behind. Thinking this through with students is important in their understanding of the power they have to shape both what a reader sees and what a reader is left to imagine.

SECOND: IMITATE

I start by making a list of moments from my middle school years, flipping through photo albums or other forms of memorabilia to get a feel for that time again. Of course, today's students have a phone full of photos to reference.

As I write, I can't remember every detail, so my writing becomes a combination of fiction and nonfiction. When capturing memories in writing, stay true to the most important part of the story. For example, if your grandmother taught you to knit, and you remember a bit of a conversation with her, write it down because that's the truth of the moment. The color of her dress? The weather outside? You can invent details like that to make the scene come to life, but you can't change what actually happened with your grandmother and call it the truth. Readers expect honesty. At the same time, readers understand that memories change over time. "A memory is not simply an image produced by time traveling back to the original event—it can be an image that is somewhat distorted because of the prior times you remembered it," said Donna Bridge in the *Journal of Neuroscience* in 2012. "Your memory of an event can grow less precise even to the point of being totally false with each retrieval." Whoa!

With that in mind, I feel freer to write. I look back to Gratz's writing and the details I noticed. I am not going to try and imitate every move he made, and that is important. Studying passages and naming the craft moves we see builds analytical skills. It is important work. As we study more, we learn more. As we share craft moves we notice on anchor charts, students can use the examples we collect for inspiration. But what we do next matters, too. I don't follow Gratz precisely, imitating everything line by line, because imitating that closely would be plagiarism.

I imagine myself at morning basketball practice in the gym of my middle school. I see myself in that moment and create a scene.

> *The cement wall was cold against my head and neck and my legs crossed, uncrossed, stretched, and bunched up. I pulled my long, blonde hair back into a ponytail.*
>
> *"David." Kirk said it with authority; he always picked him first. The repetition was reliable at least: everyday Kirk and Bobby were captains, David and Alan were first picks.*
>
> *"Alan."*
>
> *See? Told you.*
>
> *There was barely a pause as Keith-Aaron-John-Matt-Billy-Eddy- and even Ron jumped off the bench to form two packs of boys with their captains at the center of the basketball court eyeing the two girls that were left. I hated this part. More than cold lima beans on my plate at dinner or scraping wax off of our hardwood floors at home, I hated this choosing teams thing. Just once, I wanted to be captain. I'd leave Kirk and Bobby for last.*
>
> *No, I wouldn't.*
>
> *Winning was everything.*
>
> *And they were not only the cutest, most popular boys in eighth grade, they were excellent basketball players.*

Julia and I sat side by side waiting. Kirk coughed and said, "Julia," with a resigned sigh. Fair pick: she was better. Bobby just looked at the wall. He let there be a long pause, long enough for me to sit alone on that bench, color coming to my cheeks. Why did I like this boy?

"I guess we'll take Penny," he said with a groan.

All my teammates rolled their eyes.

Mr. Johnson jumped in with, "Okay boys, let's practice," firing basketballs onto the court from the rolling cart.

I did not think about craft moves as I wrote because I have internalized them after studying them for years. I use moves—such as including dialogue I remember—because I know them as elements of scenes. Our students will as well. I have seen remarkable gains in classrooms where teachers commit to the study of craft moves over time.

To demonstrate the turn Gratz makes from a scene to the history that gives context to the scene above, I draw students' attention to one paragraph from the Gratz passage:

Refugee by Alan Gratz

Ever since the Nazis had taken over six years ago, Jews were fleeing Germany. By now, May of 1939, most countries had stopped admitting Jewish refugees, or had lots of official applications you had to fill out and file and pay for before they would let you in. Josef and his family hoped to one day make it to America, but you couldn't just sail into New York Harbor. The United States only let in a certain number of Jews every year, so Josef's family planned to live in Cuba while they waited.

I show students how these few sentences fall between the scene at the station and the next one, as the train begins to move.

I think aloud with students, "This moment of waiting while teams were chosen for our morning practice was uncomfortable, and I think readers need to know why Julia and I were treated so badly by the boys and our coach. I'm going to imitate Gratz and give background information." I go back and reread the last lines and think aloud about a transition. I borrow "ever since" from Gratz to get started.

Ever since Julia's dad complained to our principal, Coach Johnson had reluctantly allowed us to practice with the boys' basketball team. It was 1975 and even though Title IX had passed three years before, it had not reached our small middle school in Portland, Oregon. There was no girls' basketball team. Julia's dad insisted they give us an opportunity to play, but no one was happy about it.

I stop and ask students if they think this is enough background information. A student asks about Title IX. I revise my writing to include information on the law and its impact on women's sports. Students always love to help with writing.

YOUR TURN

There are two choices here: one from realistic fiction and one from a horror story. Select the one you feel is a good fit for your students and use it to demonstrate scenes as building blocks in stories, as I did in the last section.

Illegal by Francisco X. Stork

The Fort Stockton Detention Center was an elementary school not too long ago. Some of the sayings meant to encourage the children are still on the walls. I was in a line with twenty women all dressed in blue jumpsuits when I read one of them:

It's nice to be important but it is more important to be nice.

Yes, but I wouldn't mind feeling a little more important to the United States. Even just a tiny acknowledgment from the government that I existed and that I was not lost in a sea of asylum petitions.

I counted the number of women ahead of me. Nineteen. There were so many of us in this school-turned-detention-center that there was always a line for everything. The worst line was for the showers, which we all needed to take at the end of a hot day. There were fourteen showers for two hundred and twenty women. A week ago, the private company that operates the detention center solved the toilet-line problem by installing ten portable toilets behind the gym, but now our outside time stinks. Another sign. This one on top of a row of yellow lockers. The picture of an angry bull inside a circle covered with a red X. Underneath it, the words:

This is a no-bullying zone.

Tell that to La Treinta Y Cuatro, the guard who made everyone's life harder than it needed to be. Yesterday she asked me if people from Mexico used toilet paper. I felt like reminding her about where her ancestors came from. She sees herself as different from the rest of us. And not only different but better. And as my luck would have it, La Treinta Y Cuatro was up ahead, doling out our job assignments. I was hoping to get one of the jobs that was advertised by the pro bono legal firm representing many of the detainees. They had put up a notice for someone who spoke English and Spanish who could help them with the interviews. But with La Treinta Y Cuatro deciding? My chances were slim to none. She didn't like me. She didn't like anybody, that was true. But she seemed to have a special something for me. Did she know what I did before I got here?

Vacancy by K. R. Alexander[56]

"You know what Saturday is, don't you?" Rohan asks.

My stomach twists with fear and excitement.

"Of course we know," Mira says. Despite the crowded lunchroom, her voice is soft. She looks down at her tray while she says it, her dark cheeks flushing in embarrassment. "You haven't stopped talking about it all month."

Rohan grins at her discomfort. Mira's right—Rohan hasn't dropped the subject since the end of November. Now, a few days before winter break, it's practically all he can talk about.

"And I'm not going to stop talking about it now," he says. He pushes his glasses back up the bridge of his nose, his brown eyes gleaming with excitement. "This[57] is our

---

[56] Recently, in a Michigan classroom, I saw three seventh graders gleefully discussing the twists and turns of *Vacancy* by K.R. Alexander. One girl had just finished it, and the other two, who had finished it earlier, were giddy that they could now discuss it together. At a nearby table, a boy said, "Stop! I'm on the waiting list. Don't ruin it." I'm not much of a mystery/suspense/horror reader, so I had never heard of this book, but if kids are signing up on waiting lists for any book in my room, I read it. Then I make sure to find a passage we can study together. Engagement is everything in teaching. And just so you know… this book is exciting, gruesome, and surprising.

[57] I want to mention a little grammar observation. When a character speaks, followed by descriptive information, followed by the character speaking again, all three elements remain all in one paragraph. I say this only because my students struggle with this. The grammar of dialogue is anything but easy, trust me. Students need lots of practice to get it right. I teach it every single year—even with college students. Don't despair, just keep teaching. Some things take a while to learn.

one chance to *finally* be among the cool kids. *No one* has ever completed the Dare. All we have to do is spend one full night in the Carlisle Hotel. That's it. If we do it, we'd be the most popular kids in Gold River, like, ever."

Mira sighs. This is the same thing he's said every day since the word spread that the seventh-grade Dare would take place this Saturday at ten. Everyone who wanted to be anyone was expected to show up and test their bravery.

"I don't know," Mira mutters.

Rohan turns to me.[58]

"What about you, Jasmine?" he asks. "Can I count you in?"

I look to Mira. She and I have spent countless nights talking about the Dare. The truth is, I don't really mind the idea of staying overnight in the Carlisle Hotel; if I'm honest, I want to know why I've always felt drawn there. But Mira is scared to death of it. Unlike me, she grew up here, which means she's grown up with all the scary stories associated with the hotel. Rumors that it never reopened because a bunch of people had mysteriously died there. Or that it's haunted. Or cursed. That it still craves human souls and will snatch up anyone brave—or stupid—enough to step foot there.

That's the whole point of the Dare: Around here, kids believe that if you stay a full night, you'll never be allowed to leave.

---

[58] Another thing about dialogue that I mention to students: Rohan doesn't say a word, but he still gets his own paragraph! I tell them, it's as if the camera moves from person to person in this conversation, and with each move, it is a new paragraph because it is a new person. Rohan's "response" to Mira is to look at Jasmine, so it counts as part of the dialogue. And you ask: *How is anyone EVER supposed to learn all these rules?!* I say, hmmm. I like a challenge, so I try.

Their Turn: Independent Practice

I am scanning my classroom during independent reading time, and I see 25 heads bent over 25 books. Ah, the joy of student engagement. No matter which novels students are reading, there are scenes. You can deepen understanding of this craft move by encouraging students to be scene collectors.

Perhaps pass out sticky notes at the start of the week and ask each student to flag a page with a compelling scene. Then make copies of those scenes and post them across a board, and have students annotate them on their own or in pairs. What craft moves do they notice? This work will spark book talks because the examples, presumably, will come from so many different books. It will also give you a lot of information on what students are understanding.[59]

[59] Bob Probst taught me this instructional move: When students annotate their thinking on posters, the teacher circulates and listens to the conversations. What do students notice? What do they miss? When you bring students back together, share these observations.

TEACHER INDEPENDENT PRACTICE: WRITE A FEW SCENES

Take no more than 15 minutes for each of these writing activities.

1. Think about a *place* that is important to you. Imagine yourself there. Write about a moment in time there. Write quickly—more quickly than the editor that lives inside you, as my friend Don Murray counseled me. When you feel you've come to the end of what you want to say, move on.

2. Think of a *person* that matters a great deal to you. Write about a moment with that person. Write the first thing that comes to your mind. Don't wait to land on the "best or most important" moment, any moment will do. Just write. Free yourself to find the next line and the next.

3. Think of an *object* that matters to you. Hold it in your mind. I think of a heart-shaped rock I keep in my jewelry box. My son found it in a stream and handed it to me once while we were hiking. I remember that moment in time and begin writing. Choose something that matters to you and write.

When you're done, read your three writings and choose the one that has the most heat for you—the one you want to expand on or fiddle with. Go back and start shaping it line by line. Spend 10 minutes or more simply improving that scene.

Reflect on what you learned from this practice. How will it influence your teaching tomorrow?

 TIP

Take Scenes to the Next Level

We deepen students' understanding of scenes and how they move in a story by teaching them the craft move described in Chapter 7: Capturing Movements in Time. I show you how to build a story, beginning with a storyboard—an effective planning and organizing tool that works across genres—one that I've found is especially helpful to those learning English.

Chapter 6

Crafting Voice

"The wire that stretches from writer to reader is singular. The writer creates in solitude, and the reader reads in solitude. Each is unknown to the other but, nonetheless, an intimate relationship is formed."

—Dani Shapiro, *Still Writing: The Perils and Pleasures of a Creative Life*

The voice of a text has power. Writing is, after all, talk. There is a human being behind every text, someone speaking to *you*. Writers craft the voice to draw us near or to create distance—to propel a plot and illuminate a character. It is not just *what* is said, but *how* it is said that tells us what is important in each scene and distinguishes one character from another.

You can hear voice in nonfiction as well. In an editorial, the writer's voice might express amusement or curiosity or anger. A memoir might be filled with sorrow or celebration—or both—and we feel the difference through voice. All writers have many voices, and they choose them based on their intent. When we study voice, we see how expansive it is across texts, whether it's a book, a poem, or an essay. We empower ourselves with the knowledge and language to help students to name the subtle differences in voice as well.

Too often, we teachers sort voice into two categories: formal and informal. Or "academic" and "everything else." I was guilty of this. In my third year of teaching, I was given a five-point checklist, including voice, for grading student work. I understood organization and editing, but voice? I told my nine-year-olds that their writing should "sound like them," because I didn't know how else to explain voice in writing. I have learned so much since then, primarily from the volume of reading I do and my curiosity for how texts work. Likewise, my students have learned so much more because of what I've learned.[60]

The first time I read *The Sky Is Everywhere* by Jandy Nelson, I found myself copying line after line into my notebook. It's been 12 years since that reading,

---

[60] As you know, our best intentions as teachers can be stymied by a lack of knowledge. Thanks for being on this journey to learn more with me.

and I've read the book several times since then just to live in Nelson's voice and language. The young teen in this novel has lost her older sister suddenly. She describes grief as "an impulse to write all over the orange walls—I need an alphabet of endings ripped out of books, of hands pulled off of clocks, of cold stones, of shoes filled with nothing but wind." Each item in the list is a precise symbol of loss. Combined, the items weigh us down; we feel the teen's loss. The voice shows us how she sees the world now that her sister is gone, and she communicates not just in words, but in the rich images those words evoke. This point of view is personal and raw, as if we have our hands pressed on her heart and feel its struggle to beat. Later she expresses her need for a new way to speak: "I need a new alphabet, one made of falling, of tectonic plates shifting, of the deep devouring dark."[61] There is power in this voice.

Often, when writing, our first instinct is to explain, to *tell*, which comes from our natural storytelling voice. We summarize and shortcut what happened. We race to the end, forgetting that essential lesson for writers: to show, not tell.[62] By studying the way an emotion, such as grief or joy or confusion or impatience, can be revealed in both voice and images, we give students a vision for what *showing* is. It makes you want to start writing, doesn't it?[63]

6a Craft Voice in Fiction and Nonfiction

FIRST: NOTICE

I hope you read the entire micro mentor text in the left column before you look at my analysis in the right column in order to experience how the voice changes from start to end. This is brilliant writing and a perfect mini-lesson text to explore voice.

---

[61] You know, in just two sentences, this book is extraordinary. You must have it!

[62] Although it is a cliché, I have revised this phrase in my teaching. I tell students writing is built on show *and* tell. I discussed this in Chapter 5—sometimes you slow down the action to show the details, and sometimes you speed past days or years to get to the next important part. If you *show* everything, the text crawls, and readers often lose interest.

[63] Go ahead. Go write. This book will still be here when you get back. Don Graves told me, "You have stories to tell that no one can tell but you." I remind myself of that and reach for my notebook.

"Model Home" from *Alone*[64] by Megan Freeman	Details I Notice
One afternoon we leave the bike and hike to the far side of the creek trail. Wander through a half-built neighborhood development left unfinished. Foundations surround gaping cellars. Skeleton frameworks of ghost houses, waiting for walls and windows. At the end of a cul-de-sac one solitary, finished house with a sign out front: MODEL HOME. A model home for model families. A fist clenches in my chest. Catches me off guard. My ears thrum.	• At this point in this novel in verse, readers know that the character has been living alone (with a left-behind dog) for months after the entire town was evacuated. Thus, the setting of her hike is quiet, even though the text doesn't say this, because we carry the absence of all humans inside of us from reading the pages before. The opening stanza evokes peace through the verb *wander*. • Two short sentence fragments define what *unfinished* and *half-built* mean. • The personification[65] of the framework haunts us with ghosts and a skeleton. • The tone shifts with *clenches in my chest*. • *A high-pitched cicada call of blood rushes through my brain.*[66] This is the feel of a 0–60 mph rush of anger. Part of our comprehension of the character's feelings is in the detail and comparison here, but the sentences have also shifted. She speaks in shorter, more direct lines. The peace of the first stanza is replaced by the repetition of *going to throw up*.

[64] In case you're unfamiliar with it, the Nerdy Book Club is an enormous community of teachers and librarians who love reading, founded by Donalyn Miller and Colby Sharp. Each year a committee votes on the best books of the year, by category. I found *Alone* because of the "2021 Nerdies: Poetry and Novels in Verse" blog post. I admit, I order everything on their lists because they choose so well (but don't tell my spouse).

[65] I struggle to keep the craft moves separate when writers blend them in sentence after sentence with such obvious delight. Here we have the frame of the house coming to life, personified in "waiting," and the metaphor of ghost houses with skeleton frameworks (so smart to juxtapose those two images in one phrase!), and then… even more! There's the alliteration of "w" in *waiting for walls and windows*. But this is my adult brain, which is fascinated by writer's craft moves. If I take this one stanza apart into too many pieces, I risk losing the sense of the whole of this passage.

[66] I recommend cicadamania.com to hear this. I've not read a description of an internal shriek as effective as this before.

"Model Home" from *Alone* continued	Details I Notice

A high-pitched
cicada call of blood
rushes through my brain.
 	
    queasy
    lean forward
    hands on knees
    going to throw up
    going to throw up
    going to throw up
    but then
    maybe not
    maybe just soul-sick
    sick-and-tired sick
    spit-in-the-dust sick
 	
Model Family my ass.
 	
Two-dimensional sticker families
on the back windows
of minivans, jeering at
the divorced kids riding behind them
in the car-pool line.
 	
Stick figures brandishing
totems of ecstatic idiocy—
coffee cups and golf clubs
soccer balls and pom-poms
	• I love the turn from "throwing up sick" to *soul-sick*. The hyphen indicates a combined meaning and is repeated with two more examples.
	
	• The voice is hard-edged but sassy in *Model Family my ass*. I would describe the shift in voice here from the broken lines when she is barely able to speak because she is overwhelmed by her anger (*queasy, leaning forward*) to the hard-edged acceptance of it in one four-word sentence. This moves to her explanation of and commentary on a Model Family. She moves from rage to reasoned argument.[67]
	
	• The shift to *sticker* from *sick* feels right because of the echo in sounds.[68]
	
	• We've all driven behind a van with a sticker family, but how many of us would describe it as *jeering*? This is the voice and experiences of our narrator. We read this world through her eyes, even if our experiences are different. However, many students will find solace in these words because being a stepkid is their experience, and they will bring that to this text.[69]
	
	• *brandishing totems of ecstatic idiocy* is quite a phrase. Each word chosen intentionally to create the perspective of the speaker.

---

[67] My college students have few words to describe the many voices they hold inside of them. They know they are there, but few see how the words and sentence lengths they choose can show rage or reasoned argument. They haven't studied this. They have never tried to be playful in a reasoned argument. This passage allows them to learn from the differences in language and in voice, and then to be able to apply both to their own arguments, stories, and editorials.

[68] That's the use of a literary device called *consonance*. See craft move 7.

[69] If you haven't explored the work of Louise Rosenblatt, brilliant thinker, and researcher, please do. She describes well why two readers see the same text differently and will thus interpret and understand the text differently. We bring ourselves to every text we read. We can't help it.

Where is the sticker stepkid
with her sticker suitcase?
Hauling between sticker weeks
back and forth
between sticker houses?
Subdividing the twenty-four hours of
sticker Christmas between
four sticker adults and
two sticker street addresses?

A truly model home would need
twice the number of bedrooms
for half the number of children.

I belong to a family
all by myself:
the only intersection
between four parents
who try to make peace
as if peace is a pie
that can be baked
sliced and served at
progressive dinners
rotating the children
from table to table
house to house.

I pick up the heaviest rock I can find
and hurl it through the big front window.

The splintering crash is almost
satisfying.

Details I Notice

- The list that follows *idiocy* defines the *totems*. The dash is used to say, "Here's what this phrase means in visual images."

- The repetition of *sticker* literally sputters throughout the next stanza. It is repeated like it is stuck in the throat of the speaker. Repetition with intention.

- The juxtaposition of *twice* and *half* makes us reread. Is the math right? What *does* that mean exactly?

- The colon is used to say "which means," and in this case, this is what it means to be in *a family all by myself.*

- The momentum in this last stanza is accomplished by the long run-on sentence following the colon. We rush through because without punctuation we are breathless when we reach the end.

- She *hurls* the rock, which echoes being ill earlier in this passage. It completes the rage felt early on with an action that is *almost satisfying.* It is a fitting end to this moment. We don't need to see her walk away.

- *Splintering, crash,* and *satisfying* are all words that have sharp sounds like glass breaking, but the voice in *almost satisfying* helps this line land softly. As if the narrator has reached a resolution, and perhaps a bit of peace, and can walk away from the blistering anger felt moments before.

SECOND: IMITATE

I look back at the text and write the first phrase in my notebook: *One afternoon*... and I stop. I can't think of a subject. I imagine one possibility: hikes I've been on with my husband, my daughter, and our dog. I see *hike* in the first stanza, and the *we* is the narrator and her dog, so I'm sure that's where the idea came from. But this isn't a subject I want to write about this morning. I look at the blank page. It is hard to start with nothing to say. I think of sewing, running, reading, bike riding... but nothing feels rich enough.

Writing is a struggle today, and that reminds me of how important it is to think aloud with students and show them how I work through struggles all writers face. Choosing a subject this morning is difficult, I think, because I'm overthinking "imitation." Sometimes we stand closely to a text and imitate it line by line, but sometimes we need more freedom than that as writers. We need both practice in imitating a micro mentor text and practice in crafting sentences, period. The first phrase of this micro mentor text invites imitation. I can think of 10 ways to add to the phrase "One afternoon." I model this early in the school year to show students how I discover subjects *as I write*. Remember, during the imitation phase, we are not seeking "finished" products. We are seeking a spark of an idea to follow. The precise language in "Model Home" inspires me to write, to play with sound, but not necessarily to write about a house or even to *complete* something.

Peter Elbow's extensive research on freewriting has helped me understand why we should start writing, even when we don't know what to write. We might list what we see in front of us or just put words to the first idea that comes to us. When we put a pen to a page, it ignites our brain to transform words into sentences... and suddenly ideas come.[70] Today, it is more effective to *write* my way to ideas than to sit and think, waiting for ideas. So, I begin with the first words that come to me:

---

[70] Yes, this research was done on pen-to-page writing, not keyboard writing. Technology is efficient and clean, but it is also distracting. Our habit is to zip from one thing to the next once we sit at a computer, not to focus on one word at a time. All writers benefit from both writing in notebooks and writing on a computer. We must remember they serve different purposes and affect our composition process.

One afternoon
when the snow
has just settled
and the sky blinks
a pale blue
between the tall,
quiet trunks of trees,
Pat says, "Put on
your boots—it's beautiful
out. Let's walk JuJu."

I look back at our micro mentor text for inspiration of something to try next, now that I have a setting established. The narrator is angry, but I'm not. I decide to focus on snow and play with sounds I hear, as I continue my walk with my dog and husband.

Our boots crunch-crunch-crunch
in the wide paths left by a snowplow.
Our road is white on white,
snow on snow,
Julius leaps into the banks
and buries his nose,
then looks up,
snout brushed in white,
ears attune to the wind...
he dashes ahead.

You probably notice that my imitation is nonfiction. Although the micro mentor text is fiction, I use the author's words to inspire my own true story. Story is story. The same techniques in crafting voice apply to both fiction and nonfiction. I am not trying to imitate *all* the elements of voice that Freeman applies in this passage. I chose playful language and shaped my experience with that voice.

Our students understand such nuances in voice because they are masterful at listening for and using nuances in daily conversation. They understand that voice is about much more than words alone, as they listen to friends, family, and, yes, teachers. They understand intuitively variations in voice, so we give them language to apply that understanding to their writing.

YOUR TURN

Because crafting a voice is tricky, I need several passages to study with students. I've collected several below, so that you can craft a number of mini-lessons.

Sunrise Over Fallujah by Walter Dean Myers

A lot of guys were getting nervous thinking we were going into combat, but most were just excited. It's funny, but as much as guys talk about not wanting to be in a danger zone, I think we really do want it. We want to get home safe, but we want the danger. We were shown films of the first Gulf War over and over, watching planes hit small targets with guided missiles, hearing the voice-overs of guys cheering. I knew we were building up to it. It was almost like getting ready for a basketball game, reassuring ourselves that we were cool, that we were going to win.

The Sky Is Everywhere by Jandy Nelson

When I play,[71] it's like I'm all shoved and crammed and scared inside myself, like a jack-in-the-box, except one without a spring. And it's been like that for over a year now.

What do you do when the worst thing that can happen actually happens? When you get that phone call? When you miss your sister's roller coaster of a voice so much that you want to take apart the whole house with your fingernails?

How will I survive this missing? How do others do it? People die all the time. Every day. Every hour. There are families all over the world staring at beds that are no longer slept in, shoes that are no longer worn. Families that no longer have to buy a particular cereal, a kind of shampoo. There are people everywhere standing in line at the movies, buying curtains, walking dogs, while inside, their hearts are ripping to shreds. For years. For their whole lives. I don't believe time heals. I don't want it to. If I heal, doesn't that mean I've accepted the world without her?

---

[71] The character is referring to playing a musical instrument.

Illegal by Francisco X. Stork

It would be a half hour or so before we reached a Border Patrol checkpoint. I put my hand over my abdomen to still the nervous cramps that I was getting. Small pieces of straw somehow found their way to my armpits. Drops of perspiration rolled from the top of my head down my forehead and into my eyes. I knew it wasn't the heat that caused the perspiration. You are afraid, that's what you are. Speaking to myself was another sign of fear.

Duke Ellington by Andrea Davis Pinkney

One by one, each cat took the floor and wiped it clean with his own special way of playing. Sonny Greer pounded out the bang of jump-rope feet on the street with his snare drum. A subway beat on his base drum. A sassy ride on his cymbal. Sonny's percussion was smooth and steady. Sometimes only his drumsticks made the music, cracking out the rattly beat of wood slapping wood.

Hurricane Child by Kacen Callender

My ma's voice is rough and low. When she speaks to strangers on the telephone, they call her "sir." I guess it must be surprising to some people, the way her voice sounds, because she's so beautiful—just about the prettiest woman you've ever seen—but I think it suits her just fine. I love the way her rough voice vibrates through the air like a beat on a drum. She sings around the house. Under her breath, since people say her voice is so ugly all the time.[72]

---

[72] I love how this passage deepens my thinking about the voice of Ma. First there is a declaration in two adjectives, then how others react to this voice and why it surprises them. But then the description slows down, and is told with beauty and gentleness, as a child would describe her mother's voice—especially when you realize a few pages later that her mother has left. This is the first paragraph in the novel, and once I'd read it, I couldn't stop until I finished.

6b Craft Voice in Letters

FIRST: NOTICE

In the chart below, in the column on the left, is a short passage from *Sunrise Over Fallujah* by Walter Dean Myers. This is followed by a second letter from this same novel that is written to a different character. I would give students both letters and have them study voice by comparing how the voices are different.

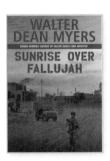

Sunrise Over Fallujah by Walter Dean Myers	Details I Notice
Dear Uncle Richie, *When I was home on leave I reread the letters you sent from Vietnam to my father. In one of them you said you were always a little nervous once you arrived in country. We're not in Iraq yet, but that's the way I feel, kind of jumpy. At one of our orientations (and we have at least two a week) an officer said that guys who fought in Nam wouldn't even recognize today's army. We're supposed to be so cool and well-trained and everything. I hope so. I was thinking that maybe your eyes wouldn't recognize today's army but I bet your stomach would.* *I can't tell you where we are right now, but it's less than a hundred miles from the Iraq border. What our army should do is take photographs of all military stuff we have over here and then send copies to the Iraqis.*	• This is the first chapter in the novel, and it begins opposite a map of Iraq. Both give the novel authenticity: This is a real place, and this could be a real letter from a soldier there. • A letter home from war feels intimate. We might imagine pages of handwriting—and you could show students images from the internet of soldiers' letters home from Vietnam. However, whether on email or handwritten, the voice here is intimate: one soldier to one soldier in conversation, as in the phrase *maybe your eyes wouldn't recognize today's army but I bet your stomach would.* My curiosity rises. • A personal letter allows the author to reveal the inner thoughts of the narrator like a secret. We understand the character's backstory—where he came from and how he got here.

That would end things right then and there. I really think the Iraqis will back down at the last minute and hand over their weapons and we'll just have to put in a handful of military police to take care of business while the political people do their thing. I don't expect anybody to be shooting at us.

You were right, though, when you said I would have doubts about my decision to join the army. You joined a war that had already started; I thought this would be different. Dad was still mad at me when I left and it was no use telling him how I felt. You know he had all those plans for me to go to college and whatnot. I tried to explain to him that I didn't think he was wrong about college or even about me studying finance. You know your brother so you know what he said—"If I'm not wrong, then why are you joining the army?" Uncle Richie, I felt like crap after 9-11 and I wanted to do something, to stand up for our country. I think if Dad had been my age, he would have done the same thing. He was thinking about me and about my future—which is cool—but I still need to be my own man, just the way you were at my age.

Details I Notice

- The choice of genre (letter) is a craft move. This letter voice is different from the voice of Robin as he narrates the scenes throughout the novel. This novel is constructed as multi-genre, meaning more than one genre is used to tell the story.[73]

- The letter is written in italics to show that it is different than the story, and it is also a different font than the character uses when writing letters home online in the story. This is a craft move meant to ease understanding for a reader.

- The best way to teach conventions is with a passage from a book—drawing students' attention to the use of them while also showing their meaning. This practice directly transfers to their personal reading when they will be more likely to notice conventions you have shown them in class.

- One focus could be paragraphing. How did Robin decide when to start a new paragraph? I have students gather around this text with a partner and name what each paragraph is about or its purpose in just a few words. We want students to understand the decisions writers make.

---

[73] Tom Romano's *Blending Genre, Altering Style* remains my go-to book for understanding how to lead students to write multi-genre texts. It is exciting, complex work for any classroom.

Sunrise Over Fallujah continued	Details I Notice

Anyway, say hello to everybody for me. And if you happen to speak to Dad, please put in a good word for me. All my life I never went against him until now and I really feel bad that he's upset about me joining. Uncle Richie, I remember listening to you and one of your buddies talking about Vietnam in your living room. You were both kind of quiet as you spoke, as if you were talking about some secret thing. That was interesting to me. I hope that one day I'll be talking and laughing the same way about what Jonesy (a guy in my unit from Georgia) calls our adventure.
   Well, that's all for now,
   Your favorite nephew, Robin
	• Parentheses are used (in both cases)[74] to add additional information without breaking the flow of the sentence. The dash (—*which is cool*—), however, adds emphasis. It tells readers to pause and take in that additional information. I always teach these two moves together, so students can see the difference, and this is a perfect text for that teaching.

Sunrise Over Fallujah by Walter Dean Myers	Details I Notice
Hey Mom! *Go on with your bad self getting online. I'm really proud of you. I know you go down to the Countee Cullen[75] branch with Mrs. Lucas to use their computers but be careful at night. Okay—so first thing, thank you for the dolls. Everybody in the church must have donated one. We gave them out to the girls just north of the Green Zone—the safe zone here. And, just as you said in your letter, the little Arab girls really went for the Black dolls. These little Iraqi girls are very sweet. Please*	• This letter home comes late in the novel, and more importantly, directly after a funeral for a soldier in Robin's company who is killed on the road in front of him. That context matters since this letter carries only the character's surface concerns. A reader of the novel will recognize the shift in tone and will understand its purpose. • The letter is meant to ease the worries of his mother, and the tone (carefree, cheerful) contributes to this, as do the events he chooses to relate.

---

[74] You see what I did there, right?

[74] Countee Cullen was a central voice in the Harlem Renaissance. I love the way Myers drops his name here, perhaps to spark a young person's curiosity, which might lead to exploration of Cullen's poems. "Incident" always breaks my heart.

thank everybody from the church for me. Jonesy is taking some pictures and I'll get some printed up for you as soon as I can.

If we weren't at war with these people this would be a great place to spend some time. You would really be impressed by the mosques. If you saw the one up at Kazimayn it would take your breath away.

Second thing—the women in Iraq mostly don't wear veils. They dress like ordinary business people. Sometimes you see women in veils but they're often from another part of the Middle East. They do cover their hair and mostly don't wear makeup. In a video store they sell tapes of belly dancers and every guy over here has at least one tape. Except me, of course, since I'm not interested in wriggling ladies. Okay, maybe just not wriggling Iraqi ladies. Did you know they also have Christians over here and a Christian church? According to the locals it's no big deal.

I can't always get online but now that you're on I'll try to find an in and email you as much as possible. Much love to you and Pops.

Robin

- The salutation creates intimacy. In the previous example, the salutation is formal. Here, it is as if we've landed in the middle of an ongoing conversation. The exclamation point conveys excitement—the thrill of connecting after a long time.

- The first phrase *go on with your bad self* is a snicker, a nudge and a smile—an intimacy between speaker and reader. Knowing the context, it is Robin reminding his mom (and perhaps himself) that he is still the same young man she sent to war. When you see this in the context of this entire novel, you can feel how hard the speaker is working to make his voice carefree so as not to worry his mother. Voice carries intent—it imagines the impact of each word on the reader.

- The phrase *wriggling ladies* downplays the intent of belly dancer videos, which feels authentic in a letter from a young man to his mom. Even word choice communicates the relationship between the writer and the receiver of a letter.

SECOND: IMITATE

I know instantly that I want to write a letter to someone who will never read it: my long-deceased grandfather. Why? I have unsaid things I need to say to him. I am inspired by the character's first line to his uncle, "When I was home on leave I reread the letters you sent from Vietnam to my father." When I was cleaning out my parents' home to sell it last year, I stumbled across a large white envelope containing information left behind by my grandfather.

Dear Grandpa Sukurski,

I found the large white envelope you filled with memorabilia at Mom and Dad's house. The note on the outside said you left it with a friend for safekeeping and he called you to come and claim it when he was on his deathbed. It was passed to my mother when you died, and she saved it. Are you surprised to hear that your granddaughter found it? Did you think it would outlive you by 40 years?

You know what was inside: photographs of you and women you had affairs with over the course of your marriage; a list of the women and the dates you were involved; notes and ticket stubs and cursive writing across pages and pages that I haven't had the courage to read. Letters from them.

I knew you had affairs, but to save the evidence—to keep a list—that act revealed something about you that I didn't want to know. Were you proud? Were you simply unable to let those memories go? Did you imagine your wife and daughter finding all of this? Why would you want them to?

I know that my mom and my grandmother chased you down to Florida once to convince you to come home. Mom was about 10, pulled from school, and taken on a road trip to reclaim her father. She remembers it as a horrible time. Your wife, a single mother of three in the 1930s, didn't have many choices, I suppose. Grandma filed for divorce twice and then withdrew the petitions. She continued to fight for you. She went to the apartment of a woman in town who she knew was your girlfriend and banged on the door. She held the

screen open with her pregnant belly. The woman dropped all contact
with you immediately, and the two women became best friends.
I want to understand that story more than I want to hear yours.

So, I knew about your repeated infidelities. As a woman, I think
I blamed my grandmother more for staying than I did you for
disrespecting her so completely. So often. There was a turn the day
I found the envelope. Those photographs hardened me. I added
them to a large box that collects dust in my basement. I want to
understand where and who I come from, but so few things you've
left behind speak for you. What is the story you hoped this package
would tell?[76]

Penny

This letter presents only one aspect of my grandfather's life. As I stepped away
from writing this chapter to do errands, it occurred to me that my letter has
limitations. I have more to say.

So when I arrived home, I drafted another letter in my notebook. My voice
shifted immediately as I sought to understand the complexities of a man I
barely knew. This time I listed memories from my childhood.

Dear Grandpa,

I remember the gardens around your house in North Bend. There
were roses, pruned and cultivated, crawling up lattice circles that
lined the front fence. I remember the three- and four-story bird
houses you built to imitate New England country inns with tiny
shutters. They perched above ponds you dug yourself and lined
with stones, then filled with Japanese Koi. There were rows of
strawberries and towering vines of blackberries wound around
homemade lattices across the side yard.[77]

---

[76] I can't explain how important it was for me to write this. Doing so allowed me to process finding that
package by speaking directly to my grandfather. I have more to say, but this start has eased the pain
a little. It makes me want to write more letters. But as you can imagine, I wouldn't share this one
with students. How about you—what letters do you want to write?

[77] I begin with a list. You recognized that craft move, didn't you?

I was the fifth granddaughter, and you built us a whirly-gig to play on when we visited. Anchored at the center by a metal wheel, its two long limbs were painted wooden planks, so two kids could ride, and another could stand and spin them. Or one bored girl could lay stomach-down across a plank and run her feet on the worn path beneath, until there was enough velocity to let go and spin—arms and legs outstretched beneath a summer sun, listening to the birds chattering from those intricate birdhouses nearby.

At the back of the property behind the garage was your shop. I remember opening the door and creeping in, peering around the corner to the workbench expecting to see you, but the silence whispered instead. I had never been invited in, so I scanned the workbench, the cubbies that held screws and nails, the wall of windows that looked out to the side yard and settled on a vise holding pieces of a bird feeder. A glimpse of you—the man who made things. I have intricate puzzle boxes with hidden drawers. I remember the wooden dining room table and chairs you crafted for my dolls that could be packed together again into a brick. You somehow captured engineering and art in woodworking. I would love to have made something with you, Grandpa.

The pictures of me at your house at ages 7-8-9 show the spunk and curiosity (and broken arms) of my child self, climbing trees without caution, racing a bike down the enormous hill nearby, coming back scraped and tired, to spin on the whirly-gig beneath a cloud-spattered summer sky. My memories of the home you built fill me with gratitude. The imprint of your gardens somehow made those drinking years easier—you, my dad, my uncle, my cousin—the continual sloppy chaos of alcohol's stormy history in our family. Inside the house I was on edge; outside I found peace. Your gardens stilled me.

There are many ways to be a grandfather. My husband pulls our granddaughters onto his lap and reads to them. He sings Maisie to sleep with "Amazing Grace" and helps her feed our dog. He makes Mickey Mouse pancakes with chocolate chip eyes and answers all their questions with patience. You did none of those things—I can't remember a single hug and never saw you cook. You seemed unimpressed when I graduated college, the first in our family to do so.

But I will always remember that you died seated on a bench in the garden, a bag of breadcrumbs in your lap, one fist holding the next handful you would scatter to the collection of birds at your feet. The tenderness you felt for birds, for the beauty of the world, just somehow never made it to the people you shared it with. I am grateful, though, for the whirly-gig, the birdhouses, and especially, your youngest daughter, my mom.

Love,
Your granddaughter Penny

As I finish this letter, I think of the words of young adult novelist John Green from an essay in his book, *The Anthropocene Reviewed*: "I think about the many broad seas that have roared between me and the past—seas of neglect, seas of time, seas of death. I'll never again speak to so many of the people who loved me into this moment, just as you will never speak to many of the people who loved you into your now. So we raise a glass to them—and hope that perhaps somewhere, they are raising a glass to us."

For writing to be rich and real for students, we must show them how rich and real it is for us. I didn't set out to write two letters, but in doing so, I got a workout in tone and purpose at the word and sentence levels. My engagement with writing helps my students see why people write when they don't have to, as Don Graves taught me. There is joy here. But also remember, when we imitate writing with our students, we are the best writer in the room. It is our responsibility to share what we do as writers with the young people before us, so that they can discover that joy as well.

YOUR TURN

In the passages below, we meet Ike, a dog who has been sent to obedience school by his owner. Study these passages together and consider how a fictional letter might inspire similar creativity and playfulness.

On the first page, we hear the dog owner's voice in a quotation in a newspaper article, "Local Dog Enters Obedience School":

Dear Mrs. LaRue by Mark Teague[78]

Citing a long list of behavioral problems, Snort City resident Gertrude R. LaRue yesterday enrolled her dog, Ike, in the Igor Brotweiler Canine Academy. Established in 1953, the Academy has a history of dealing with such issues.

"I'm at my wit's end!" said Mrs. LaRue. "I love Ike, but I'm afraid he is quite spoiled. He steals food right off the kitchen counter, chases the neighbors' cats, howls whenever I'm away, and last week while I was crossing the street he pulled me down and tore my best camel's hair coat! I just don't know what else to do!"

Dear Mrs. LaRue by Mark Teague

Dear Mrs. LaRue,

How could you do this to me? This is a PRISON, not a school! You should see the other dogs. They are BAD DOGS, Mrs. LaRue! I do not fit in. Even the journey here was a horror. I am very unhappy and may need something to chew on when I get home. Please come right away!

Sincerely,

Ike

---

[78] A book of letters and newspaper articles that tell the story of a dog that is sent to obedience school by his owner. Even though it's been 20 years since it was originally published, this book is a treasure. The illustrations show the same scene as imagined by the dog and the owner, with many details that move a reader's understanding beyond the text. This is a great K–8 book-club text because it ignites so much discussion. And now, can you imagine writing in the voice of one of *your* pets?

Their Turn: Independent Practice

Letters matter. They have always mattered. Once handwritten letters connected people across oceans. Now emails can bridge distances in minutes. Text messages take the form of mini letters: *I love you. I miss you. How are you?* Letters carry that intimacy. They allow us to reach across towns to connect with cousins or reach across time, as I have done, to speak to someone long gone.

There are many ways you might move students to practice letter writing independently.

Letters to the editor allow voices to rise from all corners of a community. They remain a staple in newspapers and magazines, and a study of those voices (written for a general audience) is a smart next step in your teaching. I've led students to write letters to former teachers, to grandparents, to siblings. We've written to political candidates. Sixth graders wrote letters to the editor of our local newspaper, and several were published. I remember one girl waving the newspaper and yelling as she ran down the hall to class the next morning, "It's my letter! I'm published!"

Nancie Atwell introduced the idea of literary letters in her worldwide bestselling book on her middle school classroom, *In the Middle*.[79] This book transformed my teaching, and I imitated many of Atwell's practices. My students wrote letters to other students in class about the books they were reading. (Not all the books they read, of course, but one each quarter.) The voice in those letters was gossipy, friendly, and thoughtful, and they often led to a deeper analysis of the books.

On my desk, for all 34 years I spent teaching K–12, I had a small white mailbox with *Mrs. Kittle* written on its side. I told students that if they had something to say to me, they could put it in writing, drop their note in the box, and raise the red flag that was attached to it. Students wrote to me for a variety of reasons: to let me know when a pet died, when they had an upcoming performance,

---

[79] I read all three editions. What a book. What a teacher.

and when their team had an important game. They wrote me questions they were too embarrassed to ask in class—about homework problems, about conflicts with friends, and even about issues connected with growing up, such as menstruation. They wrote to tell me the things that mattered to them but might be lost in the rush of a school day. That little white mailbox now sits on my daughter's desk in her fifth-grade classroom, and when I visit her, I always leave a note. And I put the flag up.

We all move fast today. It is natural that students write texts instead of emails to friends and family. Letters have all but disappeared. Students will discover the purpose and power of letter writing if you dedicate time to the study of letters and then invite them to write their own. Even today. After all, it was just a few years ago that I asked my seniors in high school to leave a letter for their parents when they moved out to attend college. I still hear stories about those letters when I see their parents in town.

There is a voice in everything we write, regardless of genre. I hope this study will lead you and your students to understand all the possibilities in letter writing.

Chapter 7

Capturing Movements in Time

"It's a wonderful feeling when you're reading something and the writer has aged exactly the right detail so that you know the story is picking up again sometime later. Sometimes the seasons change, or children start school, or beards grow long, or pets go gray."

—Anne Lamott, *Bird by Bird:*
Some Instructions on Writing and Life

7 Identify
Transitions
That Shift Time

The world is in constant motion. Even though we know each minute is the same length, some sure seem to move faster than others. Haven't you felt the need to stop time? Let me linger here, I think, as I watch my son helping his daughter roll a bowling ball or holding her hand as they walk to feed apples to goats at a nearby farm. In writing we can stop time. We can hold it in place and study a moment, revealing what's happening, but also revealing the moment's meaning for others. But then we can leap forward to imagine five years from now, or glance decades back at putting our children on the bus to school. We think in flashbacks. We imagine flash-forwards. Writers make use of both: We play with time.

I teach the power of time, using storyboards, when most writers have settled on a subject. A storyboard is a combination of sketches and words that helps the writer organize ideas and tell the story. They have been used to create films for decades. It is like conceptualizing a picture book, but instead of teaching students to devote one page to each idea, I teach them to imagine each box as a scene (see Chapter 5: Developing Scenes).

We create our storyboards in notebooks or on notecards or sticky notes. The natural buzz emerges as we create together. Students connect scenes by talking with one another. They revise their thinking as they work, often by listening to others. They consider new ways to organize scenes. Students might delete some of the scenes they've created. They might realize they have forgotten something and add it. This revision work continues as drafting begins. It is a natural part of the writing process.

My understanding of storyboards was deepened by reading *Visual Tools for Differentiating Reading and Writing Instruction* by Roger Essley and his coauthors, Linda Rief and Amy Levy Rocci. These authors worked in public schools in New Hampshire and used this strategy on everything from preparing third graders for standardized tests to helping tenth graders capture character development in *Romeo and Juliet*.[80]

Once we have a few scenes, we imagine moving them around like pieces in a puzzle. What if you move this scene to the start? How does that change the flow and momentum of your story? This is art: gratifying, sustaining, and completely engaging. Sometimes we need to step back from skills and think about our big goals for a piece of writing. We want students to be flexible writers who craft their experiences into art. We want deep thinking. We must get out of the way and encourage students to solve their own problems as they work, so they gain the confidence to plan and revise structure without us. I've seen that happen when I show students the power of storyboards to capture movements in time.

7 Identify Transitions That Shift Time

FIRST: NOTICE

In the chart on the next page, in the column on the left, is a short passage from *Illegal* by Francisco X. Stork. The author paints a memorable moment. Can you see the shift in time?

Try to name a few craft moves you see *before you read* "Details I Notice" in the box I've filled in on the right.

---

[80] My use of storyboards is a bit different from theirs, but making an idea one's own is the essence of professional learning. When you read any professional book, you imagine working with your own students. As you read this book, you will likely transform my ideas by combining them with your own. Maybe you'll even write about them so that I can learn from you!

Illegal by Francisco X. Stork	Details I Notice
The mention of the wall made me think of the place on the Rio Grande where Sara and I had crossed into the United States. After we crossed the shallow Rio Grande, we climbed a rocky ledge and stood for a moment to look at the scattered adobe houses that made up the town of Boquilles. There was a dirt road that crossed through the center of the town and ended at the edge of the river. That's where I last saw Brother Patricio. He was waving goodbye, or a blessing, or both.	• The phrase *made me think of* makes it easy to shift from the present to the past. • The author helps us see what the narrator remembers with the details that follow. The moment would have little impact if not for those details that slow down time. We stand and look back with the characters and see Brother Patricio waving goodbye. • This flashback is just four sentences.

SECOND: IMITATE

This imitation feels easy. Stork offers one sentence to launch the flashback, followed by four sentences to show the place or the moment in time. I try out some ways to start by showing my students the following sentences in my notebook. As I read each one, I fill in the blank with a word or phrase.

The mention of _____ made me think of.... "The mention of Cheetos made me think of..."

The smell of _____ made me think of.... "The smell of paint made me think of..."

The sound of _____ made me think of.... "The sound of the ice cream truck made me think of..."

The _____ made me think of.... "The sunset made me think of last summer..."

I ask my students to take a moment and finish each sentence with their own examples. I encourage them to continue writing when they hit on a word or phrase that sparks a feeling, a moment, or a possibility for writing. I write while they do:

The sound of the ice cream truck reminds me of the house on Boise Street. Cam has leapt to his feet and run for the front door. He calls over his shoulder, "Grandma, I'll stop the truck; you bring the money!" and sprints down the stairs, the screen door banging behind him. My mom and I look at each other and explode into giggles. She is already reaching for her purse.

I move to the window with Cam's sister, Hannah, resting against my hip. My dad chuckles beside me. We watch Cam jostling from one foot to the other, studying the list of treats. My mom starts down the stairs, money in hand, her smile brilliant in the afternoon sunshine. I remember those days before the walker, before her falls and her broken legs, before the oxygen tank and the death of my father—when we spent weeks each summer with the windows open listening to crows, watching squirrels, and enjoying the simplicity of summer and my young children.[81]

YOUR TURN

Select a passage from the four listed below that you feel is a good fit for your students. Use the passage to identify transitions that shift time, as I did in the last section.

Illegal by Francisco X. Stork

I thought about the time Sara and I took Mami to Palacio Peking for her birthday. My mother laughed when she read the fortune in her cookie. *La felicidad te espera.* Happiness awaits you.

---

[81] And there it is again… five minutes of writing launched me back to a moment I haven't thought about in years. I'm grateful for this practice because it brought my mother and father back to me in the fullness of health. I got to relive one moment in the home they shared for decades. It feels good to remember them filled with joy. Writing transports us. It brings moments back, even those tinged with loss.

Refugee by Alan Gratz

Now, at last, when he most needed to be seen, he was truly invisible.

Mahmoud cried in exhaustion and misery. He wanted to do it all over again. He wanted to go back and stand up for the boy in the alley in Aleppo who was getting beaten up for his bread. To scream and yell and wake the sleeping citizens of Izmir so they would see him and all the other people sleeping in doorways and parks. To tell Bashir al-Assad and his army to go to hell. He wanted to stop being invisible and stand up and fight. But now he would never get a chance to do any of that. It was too late. There was no time.

Fire Becomes Her by Rosiee Thor

The halls of Ainsley Academy carried so much history, so much expectation. But the supply closet didn't ask them to be anything more than they were, letting their romance breathe in a world that had twisted it into the shape of their school days.

Over the years, they had turned it from a dusty supply closet into a small but sublime refuge from the world. In their first year, they'd hidden notes in a filing cabinet for each other, and in their second year, Linden had stolen the janitorial staff's key to the room—he'd paid them handsomely not to replace the locks—and in their third year, at the advent of their official relationship, they'd moved furniture into the space: an armchair big enough for them both if she sat on his lap, and a cheap flare lamp to see by.[82] In their fourth year, she'd bought a wall hanging, and in their fifth year, he'd replaced the flare lamp with twinkle lights. It wasn't much, but it was theirs.

---

[82] That's a 77-word sentence! Didn't you feel yourself a little breathless as you read? We might be tempted to call it a run-on, but the punctuation is all technically correct. I ask students, "Why did the author combine the three years of memories into one long sentence?" What do you think?

Clearly, we're dealing with a tripped breaker or something and the breaker box is down here, so I'm good.

I check my phone—47 percent charged. Okay, it's on the wrong side of the halfway mark, but it's not terrible. I switch the flashlight app on and head to the opposite corner of the basement, feeling my way along the walls.

Of course, this isn't my first outage—there's been a few times, usually triggered by a bad storm, where the lights are suddenly flickering and then, boom, just like that, every plugged-in thing—dishwasher, TV, fridge, the hot water heater, came to a grinding halt. And then Real Dad and I would trudge downstairs into the far back corner of the basement, where apparently the power box hangs out.

Real Dad would open the box, scan the rows of switches, find the problem child and flip it back on, issue solved and then we'd march back upstairs to the living room like the heroes we were. I'd say, "The heroes have returned and we have returned light upon this land," or something equally cheesy, and The Bronster would make fun of me. Except I didn't care what he said or thought because I knew I had provided a vital service: I was the Holder of the Flashlight, or more accurately, the Holder of the Phone with Its Flashlight App Turned On—and yeah, okay, occasionally I got a little distracted, prompting Real Dad to say, "Eddie, sorry to bother you and your shadow puppetry, but would you mind aiming some of that light at the power box so I can, you know, see what I'm doing and not get electrocuted?"—but that was the exception, not the standard!

Now I'm bumping into storage bins stuffed with our winter clothes. I'm tripping over Mom's old bowling ball. And I nearly wipe out when I tip over a jar of golf balls. Who keeps a jar of golf balls? And yeah, I feel extra abandoned down here. And, yeah, this is officially my worst nightmare, glad you could be here.[83]

---

[83] Look at all that craft in one passage: the unusual, but purposeful capital letters, the asides, the word choice, the list! Not to mention the obvious play with voice. This writer had fun writing this character's perspective.

BONUS!

If I Stay by Gayle Forman has an unusual structure. A teenager is in a brutal car accident on a snowy road in Oregon[84] and is caught between life and death. As people visit her in the hospital, Forman focuses on why each person matters to the main character, using vivid flashbacks that stretch for pages. The story takes place over 24 hours, but you travel years in that same time beside the character. The central story is a heart-pounding emergency, but the backstory slows you down, showing you why you must care.

I bet you are thinking of pairing *If I Stay* with *Long Way Down* by Jason Reynolds, aren't you? The narrator, Will, gets on an elevator to kill the young man who killed his brother. But at each floor the elevator stops, a ghost steps in. The ghost holds an important memory from Will's past. Can the ghost convince Will to break the chain?

Imagine writer's craft book clubs: solid gold.

Their Turn: Independent Practice

You don't have to teach these craft moves in order, but if you have, your students have learned a lot about how writers use details and dialogue and scenes to craft fiction and nonfiction. Much of their imitation has happened in the writing notebook. It's practice.

I don't grade practice on quality, just on quantity. Every few weeks I give students a checklist of all the craft moves we've studied, checking off the imitations they've tried in notebooks. I also ask one or more of the following questions about what they are learning:

- What are you learning about yourself as a writer with all this practice?
- Put a sticky note on an entry you would like for me to look at closely. What feedback would be helpful to you?

---

[84] Oregon is my home state; I was born and raised there. Not only do I picture every moment of this novel with unusual clarity, but I make up details for settings as I am reading based on the decades I lived there. I even imagine a particular stretch of highway for the accident. Readers bring background knowledge to what they read, and this is a perfect example of the power of that.

- What have you noticed about your moves in revising your writing?
- What patterns have you noticed in your notebook? Are there particular subjects that you write about a lot?
- What have you learned about writer's craft by studying micro mentor texts together?
- What do you still need to work on in your writing?

After months of study, I go deeper. I assess how much students can do without me. I give them a few days to find a passage in their independent-reading book that captures some of the craft moves we have studied. I give them time to read each day in class, so they have time to find a great passage and ask me for help if they need it. From there, I make copies of the passages and ask students to annotate the craft moves they notice, which enables me to assess what they see and what they don't see. I organize small groups after the assessment to reteach craft moves to those who have missed them.

The connection between independent reading and passage study is vital for all students. Over time, they'll recognize moves that some authors make across their books. I've heard students make comments such as, "That's definitely a Reynolds move. He pulls you close to a character with his inner thoughts. Like right here...." Comments like that prove a student is moving beyond following a plot to seeing the writer at work. I've watched students plan stories with their independent-reading books in their hands, imitating the author's structure or point of view. This is sophisticated and complex work, and all students are capable of it. Let's empower them and give them the freedom to compose on the shoulders of their mentors, using those mentors' tools to craft their own ideas.

Chapter 8

Using Literary Devices

"Language is the greatest tool invented by humankind. We shape our identity by defining ourselves in words; we imagine our lives and make plans with it; we use it to explain, to defend; we use it to explore and to discover. We need it to survive."

—Judith Ortiz Cofer, *Lessons from a Writer's Life*

I took my four-year-old granddaughter, Maisie, to the New Hampshire Children's Museum on a recent Friday. The ramp up to the third level is lined with paintings of dogs created by several local artists. The artists not only depict different dogs in different settings, but they also use color and bring a certain style (whimsy or kindness or wildness) to each dog that invites a closer look. Those are artistic devices. The closer we looked, the more we noticed.

The same is true with writer's craft. There are endless ways to tell a story set by the ocean or to recreate a snowy day. Endless possibilities and an array of literary devices make the act of writing irresistible.

Many students, however, experience school writing as a relentless, artless task. They follow directions, often in the form of a rubric, to staple sentences and paragraphs together, rereading those directions to "get it right" like we might reread directions when assembling a dollhouse. Students tire quickly when practicing the same thing. Effort wanes. Joy disintegrates. But when you give them many opportunities to *create*, not just comply, the act of writing simmers with possibility. Just like walking through that hallway of dogs made me and Maisie see the possibility of painting. We must show students that art in writing matters, and that they can create art using literary devices.

Consider one sentence from Andrea Yang's award-winning picture book *Watercress*:

> *"Finally, we loaded everything,*
> *the soggy bag,*
> *my sopping shirt,*
> *our sodden selves,*
> *into the car and headed home."*

To paint with words, not just to narrate or explain, brings life to Yang's sentence. We can feel music in it, not only because the list of three details is parallel in structure, but because of alliteration (a repeating consonant at the start of *soggy, sopping, sodden selves*). Even the last two words create it (*headed home*). This ordinary moment has real beauty. I imagine Yang fiddling with her sentences, knowing the power of synonyms, and adding, then reordering her list to make the most of the sounds her readers will hear when they read the sentence aloud.

Young children are attuned to sounds; they want to hear the same books read to them again and again. They mimic the patterns of language. So let's take those natural tendencies one step farther and name the devices authors use to create indelible images.

I have discussed the importance of reading at several points in this book.[85] Wide, regular reading impacts writing and, specifically, vocabulary development. To use some of the artful devices discussed in this chapter, students need a lot of words. Andrea Yang can summon adjectives that not only start with *s* but are synonyms for being wet (and uncomfortably so) because she knows a lot of words. They are not all sophisticated words, but they are accessible to her because, I am certain, she reads a lot. She likely uses a thesaurus, in addition to her word knowledge. Both resources are important for young writers, who should collect words as they read and read and read, and revise their writing using literary devices.

This study is designed to show students how literary devices enliven texts. Sentences work on us as we read them, sometimes in ways we can't articulate. But when we look at them closer, we often see the author's artful use of language.

> ## ⊙ TIP
>
> **Explore Vocabulary Collaboratively**
>
> I ask my students to devote a section of their writing notebooks to vocabulary. Then when they encounter words that interest them, they write them in that section. They also list synonyms and antonyms for words they use often. Sometimes they add words when meeting in writing groups. I might give them a common adjective (e.g., *wet, slow, unhappy, joyful*) and ask them to brainstorm synonyms together. Word power begins with collecting.

---

[85] Developing a reader's identity and individual reading life of joy, curiosity, and passion is Job #1 in the classroom. Reading makes us stronger in all things.

8 Enliven Writing With Literary Devices

FIRST: NOTICE

In the following chart, in the boxes on the left, are short passages from several books you may already have in your library. Each passage shows the use of a literary device.

What do you notice in the passage? Try to name the literary device and other craft moves *before you read* "Devices I Notice" in the column on the right.

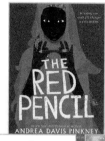

The Red Pencil by Andrea Davis Pinkney	Devices I Notice
Together we wiggled and tugged the tiny wobbly speck of white that hung tight.	• First, I hear the hard *g* sound in *together*, *wiggled*, and *tugged*. This device is called **consonance**. It means the reoccurrence of similar sounds in close proximity in a text. • Then I hear *tugged* and *tiny* followed by *wobbly*, *white*, and *tight*. This is **alliteration**. Alliteration is the repetition of the initial consonant sound in two or more nearby words. • Lastly, I hear *white* and *tight* in proximity, which is called **assonance**.[86] This is defined as the repetition of similar vowel sounds in proximity.

---

[86] Yes, you said that correctly: assonance. Just using the word—with its first three letters—in my lessons sends many students into fits of giggles. Don't you love that teaching makes you laugh sometimes?

The Red Pencil by Andrea Davis Pinkney	Devices I Notice
morning stirs…	• **Personification** is bringing human qualities to something nonhuman. The use of personification brings movement and energy to an object.

Illegal by Francisco X. Stork	Devices I Notice
A chaotic sea of concrete. As many cars as there are stars. The infinity of man-made things as we approached Aurora reminded me in a strange way of the nights in the desert under millions of stars and galaxies and unknown planets.	• A common literary device is the use of a comparison in order to deepen understanding for a reader. The most common forms are **simile** (*as many cars as there are stars*) where two objects, often unrelated, are compared to each other using "like" or "as"; and **metaphor** (*a chaotic sea of concrete*) which is also a comparison of two objects, often unrelated, but direct, whereas a simile is indirect—one object *is like* another. In metaphor, the concrete *is a* sea (in this passage).

Land of the Cranes by Aida Salazar	Devices I Notice
I remind Mami this is the land of the cranes. We have wings that can soar above walls.	• This book is a marvelous example of an **extended metaphor**, which is a repeating image that unites a text. The crane reappears in new ways, continually evolving with the story, and students love discovering this.[87]

Alice Austen Lived Here by Alex Gino	Devices I Notice
I was downstairs in half an hour, sitting on the low stone walls that bordered the walkway from the street to the front door of our building. Twenty-eight minutes, actually.	• Writers might use **repetition** intentionally to highlight an important idea, or in this example, to show the feelings of a character in a situation. The character is anxious, and by repeatedly focusing on the time, Gino conveys her feelings without saying, "The character is anxious."

[87] There is an opportunity for whole-class study here. Or perhaps for a read-aloud. I have provided other examples below for you to consider, but not all the references that occur in this gorgeous text. Consider this a treasure hunt for you and your students!

Alice Austen Lived Here continued	Devices I Notice
I couldn't blame Jess for not being there during those two minutes, but I could blame her for not being there for the eighteen more it took her to show up. Eighteen minutes that I had to wait to take the same walk I took to the bus with TJ almost every day. I could have made the trip there and back in that time….what I said when she finally appeared wasn't exactly fair, but she was late, and best friends weren't supposed to keep each other waiting if they could help it.	

Harry Potter and the Sorcerer's Stone by J. K. Rowling	Devices I Notice
In *Harry Potter and the Sorcerer's Stone*, Harry goes shopping for what he needs to take to wizarding school. He stumbles into an alley off the central shopping district. His guide, Hagrid, scolds him for this. "Skulkin' around Knockturn Alley, I dunno—dodgy place, Harry—don' want no one ter see yeh down there—" "I realized that," said Harry, ducking as Hagrid made to brush him off again.	• **Symbolism** is an important literary device that becomes increasingly important throughout a student's years in school. It is a sophisticated move since its power lies in interpretation, perception, and imagination. It is often a subtle device, as in this example. Symbolism gives abstract meaning to something concrete.[88] In this case, "Knockturn Alley" sounds like "nocturnal alley." *Nocturnal* is defined as done or occurring at night, so we feel the darkness in the word Knockturn. I often tell students symbols can be a *felt sense* as we read. When we stop to analyze why we feel a certain way, we might stumble upon symbolism.

[88] I can't imagine a better source for studying symbolism with middle school students than the *Harry Potter* series. Science fiction and fantasy are filled with symbols! A book club would give students a wonderful space to practice finding symbols because they will depend on each other, instead of you, to explore symbols and discover how their meaning develops over time.

The Dreamer by Pam Muñoz Ryan	**Devices I Notice**
As Neftalí listened to the piano of wet notes, he looked up at the Andes mountains, hovering like a white-robed choir. He looked out at the river Cautín, pattering through the forest. He closed his eyes and wondered what lay beyond, past the places of Labranza, Boroa, and Ranquilco, where the sea plucked at the rugged land.	• This lovely novel uses **irony** with the central character, Neftalí. Irony is a twist: The event or language is deliberately contrary to what we expect. In this case, Neftalí, who embodies the life experiences of famous poet Pablo Neruda, stutters. Neftalí narrates the world around him with vivid, expressive, precise language in his mind, but he is unable to speak to his father without stammering. The words of this poet are unable to be heard.

The window opened. A carpet of rain swept in and carried Neftalí to the distant ocean he had only seen in books. There, he was captain of a ship, its prow slicing through the blue. Salt water sprayed his cheeks. His clothes fluttered against his body. He gripped the mast, looking back on his country, Chile.

The screech of a conductor's whistle snapped to attention. He jerked around.

Father's body filled the doorway.

Neftalí shuddered.

"Stop that incessant daydreaming!" The white tip of Father's yellow beard quivered as he clenched and unclenched his narrow jaw. "And why are you out of bed?"

Neftalí averted his eyes.

"Do you want to be a skinny weakling forever and amount to nothing?"

"N-n-n-no, Father," stammered Neftalí.

• •

Neftalí loved the rhythm of certain words, and when he came to one of his favorites, he read it over and over again: *locomotive, locomotive, locomotive.* In his mind, it did not get stuck. He heard the word as if he had said it out loud—perfectly.

SECOND: IMITATE

The micro mentor texts above provide many opportunities for practice with literary devices. I will imitate Alex Gino's use of intentional repetition to show how a character is feeling instead of simply telling my reader how he is feeling. Gino's example is an excellent mentor for this.

First, I pick a feeling. My character is sad. How can I show that through repetition? I imagine a child departing for summer camp, reluctant to leave his room. I want to use details that show reluctance in his actions.

I say to my students, "My character is about 10 years old and packing for summer camp. I look back at Gino's passage and notice it is in the first person. That's how I'll start. The word *minutes* is a clear repetition. I am searching for a word that I can repeat while I create the scene, but I've learned it is better to start writing than to stay stuck in planning what to write. The solution to my problem may occur as I start writing."

I open my sock drawer and reconsider my choices.[89] *Should I take another pair of white socks? Will I be expected to do laundry at camp? I don't know how to do laundry. I shut the door and glance at my bed. I am under the covers before I think about it—wrapping my comforter over my head.*

Mom yells from downstairs, "10 minutes!"

I crawl out of my bed and consider the pile of shirts. Brady jersey. Maybe not a good idea. I put it back in my dresser and search for a replacement. My Little League jersey? Better. As I place it on the stack on my bed I see the last remaining strip of my childhood blanket. I still sleep with it, but I just can't see taking it to camp. What if someone sees?

---

[89] I might continue to speak to my students as I write. "I want to show the character delaying the task—doing something that is silly like making a pile of socks to take and then looking over the pile to decide whether those are the right socks to take—which you know most 10-year-olds wouldn't care about, unless they were deliberately trying to be slow." But if I do this, I give away what I am trying to make evident in the text itself, without explanation.

Bruno scratches at my door. I open it and reach down to stroke his ears. He leans against me and groans a little. "It's only a few weeks," I tell him, "You'll be okay."

Now that the scene is shaping up, I consider how to make repetition more evident. It might be through reassuring self-talk, where the character tells himself, *you'll be okay/it'll be okay*, and then tells the dog the same at the end. I go back and read my passage aloud and insert the phrase where it feels right. I always revise in a different color so students can quickly see my revisions:

I don't know how to do laundry, but it will be okay, someone will show me how.

What if someone sees? I don't think that will be okay. I am 10.
I shouldn't need my blanket at camp. And even if I do, I'll be okay without it. I bite my lip and slip my worn blanket under the covers.
It will be here when I come home.

YOUR TURN

Below, you'll find micro mentor texts from five books that contain literary devices. You could use the book as your book talk each day and study the passages below that are from that text. This will likely inspire some students to want to read the entire book.

Remember to ask students to explain why they think the author chose to use each device. We want students who can not only name the device when they see it, but can also understand why and how they might use it in their own writing.

When Marian Sang **by Pam Muñoz Ryan**

As Viola sang the high part and Marian sang the low, their harmony blended like a silk braid.

*

Finally, the girl said, "We don't take colored!" Her voice sounded like a steel door clanking shut.

A soldier cut the zip tie off Mahmoud's wrists. Mahmoud expected the relief to be instant, but instead his hands went from numb to on fire, like the tingling needles he felt in his leg after it fell asleep, times a thousand.

I was suddenly filled with an emptiness as barren and desolate as the view outside my window.

*

The school was transformed into a prison by the simple act of enclosing the building and part of the grounds with a twenty-foot chain-link fence with rolls of razor-sharp wire on top. They brought in a trailer with eight commercial-sized washers and dryers, and they built three cement-block isolation cells with small windows on the top where detainees who misbehaved could be kept. Oh, and they also installed cameras every twenty-four feet.

Papi is coming, I whisper to myself. I tuck my wings close and wait.

*

I learn someone named ICE put Papi and other hammer workers in a cage and Mami doesn't know how to set him free. I cry to think of Papi unable to fly.

*

Could I fly without Papi?

*

...I tug the cut pillow cloth up to my nose and smell the trace of his feathers in the cotton.

*

I practice flapping my feathers while I trot to keep up to Mami.

He chose an especially shiny coin, balanced it between his left thumb and his right middle finger, and set it spinning. He picked up a second and then a third, getting them going as the first tipped from a round-and-round spin to an up-and-down wobble that led to a lie-down flat with a final buzz.

*

Rick kept spinning until the quarters were scattered around him. Then he scooped them up and began again. This time he put a shiny coin into each hand and spun them both at the same time. The quarter on the right set to dancing on end, while the one on the left started wobbling right away. At least it didn't fall down immediately. When he started practicing simultaneous spins, his right hand produced nothing but wobblers, and his left hand would have gotten more movement by dropping the coin on the table with a plop.

When Marian Sang by Pam Muñoz Ryan

Audiences applauded in London, cheered in Paris, and pounded on the stage for encores in Russia.

Their Turn: Independent Practice

Your students need time to read without interruption—the way my family hikes the White Mountains. We mostly walk and talk without stopping to name the birds we hear or the kinds of trees and clouds we see. A little naming, of course, builds understanding, but we wouldn't want to miss the expansiveness of the experience by turning it into a quiz. Reading, for the most part, should be a "show, not tell" experience: Let books show your students all their treasures. Do not spend too much time naming and analyzing them.

Collecting beautiful passages from the books we read, though, is a powerful classroom practice. Since I began tweeting my own book passages I love, students at all grade levels have been sending theirs to me. Here are two collections from my writing notebooks.

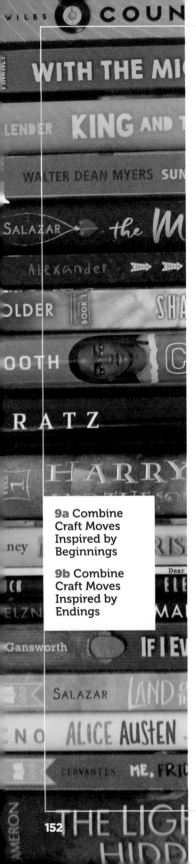

Chapter 9

Combining Craft Moves: The Power of Beginnings and Endings in Books

"I am happiest when I am rubbing two words together to produce an unexpected insight, when I feel the sentence turn under my hand, the paragraph shrink or rise until it breaks in two, the narrative flow toward rapids I can hear but do not yet see. The draft is always, for me, alive with possibility."

—Donald M. Murray, *Crafting a Life in Essay, Story, Poem*

Throughout this book I've isolated craft moves to show the importance of each one. I'm sure you've been thinking all along—*but don't authors use all of them simultaneously?* Absolutely. Just like chefs, authors combine ingredients based on what they're cooking. In this chapter, I show you how I lead students to understand the ways craft moves come together. I begin by looking at two typical elements in books: beginnings and endings. A lot happens in both.

Authors know they need to hook readers in the beginning. "First Chapter Fridays" is a popular practice to entice students to read. You read an entire first chapter of a book aloud, so that students can hear the best reader in the room (yes, you) reading with interest and enthusiasm. Because it is just the opening of a whole book, many students will want to hear you read more—or pick up the book themselves and continue reading it independently. Exactly. The book might end up on their "what-to-read-next" list.

First Chapter Fridays can also be an excellent way to bring together the craft moves we've studied in this book to deepen students' understanding of them and their connections.

Likewise, it is smart to draw students' attention to the craft moves in the endings of books. You will want to save that study until you have finished a class read-aloud or once students have finished several books on their own. That way you won't spoil a book by studying an ending before a student has a chance to read it.

9a Combine Craft Moves Inspired by Beginnings

FIRST: NOTICE

Below is the opening of *Vacancy* by K. R. Alexander. What do you notice in the passage? List your observations before you read mine.

Vacancy by K. R. Alexander	Details I Notice
I'll never forget the first time I saw the Carlisle Hotel in person. After my mom died, my dad wanted a fresh start. He kept saying he wanted to get out of the city and reconnect. With nature. With the place he and Mom had met. With me, if he could. We'd grown so distant since Mom died. I knew he wanted to reconnect with me most of all. He talked about the town all the time: Gold River. He talked about it so much that even though I'd never been there, I felt like I'd lived there my whole life. I listened to his stories. I felt the pull, too. Gold River was home—it was where I was meant to be. Which is how I ended up halfway across the country in the tiny tourist trap of a town at the base of Crossback Mountain, one of the biggest, oldest ski resorts in the area. Gold River was sprawling but quaint at the same time, perfectly made to invite in eager skiers. There were some ski-repair shops whose names I knew from the multiple applications my dad had sent in. There were cute diners and high-end restaurants to warm up in after a day on the slopes. And if the tourists wanted to rent a chalet with Swiss lattice and a steep roof, there were a few dozen to choose from.[90]	• The narrator's voice is compelling to me because of what is revealed. Right away, important details are shared, as if the narrator has pulled me close. • The use of short, direct sentences reveals a lot of information at a quick pace. • The description of Gold River begins with a list.

[90] This paragraph describes where I live precisely. Do you think the author wrote this in North Conway, New Hampshire?

There was only one place they shouldn't stay—

The Carlisle Hotel.

The Carlisle was perched at the edge of town, surrounded by pine trees and backing up to some abandoned ski runs. Huge and ancient, the size of a city block, with wood-shuttered windows and gilded front doors—the type of hotel millionaires once flocked to in droves. The type of hotel that once promised luxurious furnishings and elegant dinners and dramatic views from every firelit room.

But not anymore.

I felt my breath catch the first time I passed it. It was beautiful, but also sad and empty.

That's exactly how I felt then—sad and empty.

I had felt that way for what seemed like forever.

I stayed away from the hotel at first. Moving in August meant I could start school like everyone else. I made friends and learned my way around the town before the holiday season kicked in. In those first few weeks, the hotel wasn't the only building that felt abandoned. Only for the Carlisle, the emptiness wasn't seasonal.

Eventually the mountains got their first dusting of snow, and all the tourists flocked back, eager to get back on the slopes. The chalets filled. The shops bustled.

The Carlisle stayed vacant.

It had been that way for almost thirty-three years.

I should be honest, though: That wasn't the first time I truly saw the hotel.

I first saw the Carlisle in my dreams.[91]

Details I Notice

- The one-phrase paragraph "The Carlisle Hotel" highlights its importance. We pay attention because it sits by itself as its own paragraph.

- The description of the hotel is a list, but with more sensory details than the list that describes the town. Why do you think the author adds color and image here?

- There are several times the author uses a one-sentence paragraph to separate longer descriptions. Consider how they change the pace of the reading.

- Use of vivid verbs (*flocked, bustled*).

---

[91] Tell the truth, did you jump when you read that transition? I sure did. This narrator has me in the palm of her hand. Genius. No wonder so many students wait in line to read this book.

SECOND: IMITATE

The first chapter of *Vacancy* is 536 words—as long as a typical piece of "flash fiction," a story written in 500–750 words.[92] I have students write fiction because, as Tom Newkirk says, "Fiction writing allows for greater psychological range than do most nonfiction forms. The writer can imagine extremes of fear, anger, resentment, and yes, evil that they don't and wouldn't want to experience in real life" (2021).

"We will practice combining craft moves in our notebooks by writing fiction," I tell students. This is usually met by a flurry of energy.

I continue, "One of the best things about writing anything—including flash fiction—is knowing that whatever I put down today can be revised tomorrow. That takes the pressure off. I'm just going to start writing and try to keep going without stopping. I want to write something creepy, but I'm not sure how to."

I look back at our mentor text: *I'll never forget the first time I... walked into 6th grade. I was the youngest in my class, so maybe that's why I was so afraid I would fail math. I ...*

I pause and address the class, "I feel stuck. I look back at our micro mentor text and see the next sentence begins with *After my mom died...*" I reread what I've written above out loud and add to it:

> *I flinched as a memory from the year before returned. The fire alarm blasted the silence of math class, and I jumped with a yelp that was half surprise and half relief. Any escape was welcome. The class was on their feet and moving out of the door before Ms. Palmesano had even picked up her gradebook. But even as we rounded the corner to the stairs, we knew something was wrong. There was the screech of the alarm and the eerie screen of smoke, but we were the only students in the hall.*

"I love this!" I tell the class, "I have something mysterious to drive the rest of my story. I think I will cut the first sentences on sixth grade and jump right into fifth." I demonstrate how to use Microsoft Tools to check the word count. "That's 94 words, which means I am almost 20 percent finished, and I've barely started! I need to plan this story carefully to stay within this word count. Here's what helps me." I fold a blank page into four equal parts. "These could be four

---

[92] This is also known as "microfiction."

scenes in my flash-fiction story. In the first scene I show the smoke filling the halls. In the second scene I will show the students running out the doors to the playground and finding no one there. This is the perfect place to use sensory details. I want you to feel the quiet and the eerie sense of something very wrong happening."

I continue planning scenes in front of my students. "Perhaps the students all turn around and even the teacher is gone in scene three, just as we watch the school explode into flames behind us. I could use dialogue to show the reactions of the students. I am also going to use literary devices to describe the explosion: *as loud as... like a....*"

Remember, the goal of this lesson is not to write a perfect piece of flash fiction, but to show students the process you use to solve problems as you work to combine craft moves.

YOUR TURN

The scenes below introduce us to two characters through the actions of others. There are many craft moves in each of these passages. Select one that you feel is a good fit for your students to move their flash fiction forward. The authors combined craft moves in both of them.

The Lines We Cross by Randa Abdel-Fattah

I park my car on a side street, grab my sketchpad from under the passenger seat, and walk to Auburn Road. There are roadworks blocking all traffic. I cross the road and see a group of men hanging out together, using the fluorescent-orange traffic cones as seats.

I go to a nearby café and order some lunch. The guy who serves me is built like a tank, muscles squeezing out of his too small T-shirt, a tattoo sleeve on one arm and even a shaved head that looks muscular.

There's an outdoor table available, giving me a clear view of the street. My eyes follow the men hanging around the cones. I feel animated all of a sudden and pick up my pencil and start sketching.

Lost in my work I don't realize that the guy from behind the counter is talking to me. He places my drink on the table and, glancing at my open sketchbook, says, "You're good."

Embarrassed, I instinctively cover the page with my arm. "Nah, not really."

"You are. Can I have another look?"

He peers closely at the page and then nods, impressed. "You study art at university or something?"

"I'm in eleventh grade. This is for an assignment."

He looks at my page again and then looks over at the men. He fixes his eyes on me, his lips curled into a half smile.

"You live around here?"

I shake my head. "Nope."

"I didn't think so. So why those men?" He jerks his thumb in their direction.

I shrug. I'm not sure myself.

"Do you know them?"

"No."

"They're refugees from Sudan."

"Okay."

His tone is pleasant enough, but I feel I'm being reprimanded. That in his eyes I've done something wrong.

"Imagine I came to your side of Sydney and started sketching the natives there."

"What do you mean?" I say, a little defensively.

"A group of white women wearing matching Lululemon outfits and sipping soy quinoa shakes. In watercolor."

I feel my neck burn.

He smiles. "It's cool. I'm only mucking around with you. Enjoy your lunch."

I slowly pick at my food. I look at the sketch and close the book. When eventually I've finished eating I get up to pay the bill.

"Hey, sorry if I came across a little aggressive," he says cheerfully as he hands me my change.

"I didn't mean to offend anybody," I say.

"People usually don't," he replies, still smiling.

When I get home, I hunker down in my room and start my assignment all over again.

With the Might of Angels by Andrea Davis Pinkney

For the next question, Mrs. Ruth singled me out again. She didn't seem to call much on other kids. Some of them even wanted to answer, but I'm the one who got all the attention. And I'm the one who got slapped down every time I spoke.

"Dawnie, what is a synonym?"

Another easy question, but I thought carefully before answering. I asked myself, *Are there eight parts to a synonym?*

I said, "A synonym is a word or a way of saying something that means the same thing as another word or another way of saying something."

That was the right answer. I just *knew* it.

"Wrong, Dawnie," said Mrs. Ruth. She looked pleased to be saying those two words together. *Wrong Dawnie.*

"A synonym is a word *or expression*," Mrs. Ruth proclaimed.

Alls I could think was, *Isn't that what I just said?*

Mrs. Ruth asked, "Dawnie, are you paying attention?"

Mrs. Ruth, are YOU paying attention? This is English class, right? Are WE speaking the same language? Because I am SAYING the exact same thing you're saying, but saying it different, and forgetting just one small part. But—like a synonym—we MEAN the same thing.

Are YOU paying attention, Mrs. Ruth? Are YOU? How about if I call you Wrong Mrs. Ruth?

You are wrong for ridiculing me in front of everyone when my answer is mostly right.

I said, "Yes, ma'am, I'm paying attention."

Dear Mrs. Ruth,

I have a gift for you—a present. (In case you are not paying attention, gift *and* present *are synonyms.)*

Here are a bunch, a bundle, a heap of synonyms for how I feel about your English class:

Aggravated.

Enraged.

Furious.

Hotter than Tabasco sauce.

Mad as a hornet.

Angry as a rattler.

> *Sincerely,*
>
> *Truly,*
>
> *Honestly,*
>
> *(These are more synonyms, Mrs. Ruth.)*
>
> *Dawnie Johnson*

9b Combine Craft Moves Inspired by Endings

FIRST: NOTICE

Authors tend to craft endings differently from beginnings. In the beginning you introduce characters and the setting in what is called the exposition of the story. The ending, however, is the wrap-up. The action has come to resolution, the trouble in the story has been resolved, and many authors bring back images and ideas from throughout the novel or short story to show a change. The trees in the opening setting might be filled with spring leaves and then at the end, they are twigs against a dark sky waiting for winter. You might see the craft moves of dialogue, sensory details, or an extended metaphor used, but the author uses them to bring the story to a close. You might feel contentment for the end of a journey through the use of an extended metaphor. You may be reluctant to let go of characters because you see them so clearly in your mind. Writer's craft made that happen.

A book invites us to think about people and situations not only in the book, but also in our own world. We consider what we have learned. We finish a book in a different place from where we started. We live an experience beside characters and are transformed in some way by it. Ah, the incredible beauty of words to evoke this in us.

In the ending, the author might draw out key parts of the story to remind us of the journey we have shared. When you study a book with students, pay attention to how the ending is crafted. You'll find many craft moves come together to set the reader down with gentle, purposeful satisfaction.

Fire Becomes Her by Rosiee Thor	Details I Notice
Ingrid sighed and turned back to the group, looking at them each in turn, the faces of friendship. What could she say that would mean everything she felt? What could she say that would not take hours upon hours to craft into a perfect sound bite? Finally, she raised her glass and said simply, "To us." They all laughed, but they raised their glasses and repeated after her. Ingrid drank, letting magic run through her for the first time since she'd faced Holt. Her friends pulled her forward after the rest of the bigger and better Team Meyers on their way to usher in a new president, and Ingrid set her glass down on the porch, leaving it nearly full. Magic made her feel tired and tormented. It was a shadow of a flame dancing to the hypnotic rhythm of money, and Ingrid didn't need it to feel powerful. Not anymore. As she made her way outside and down the street, Ingrid felt the flare leave her body, little golden stars shooting from her fingertips. And as it did, she felt no less powerful, because power wasn't about who she could tear down in a ruin of flame. It was about who she could lift up, and she didn't need magic to do that. She took Alex and Charlotte by the hand and, with an aggrieved Louise tailing them, broke into a run, laughter on her breath, hope in their chests. The flutter in her veins was a little bit friendship, a little bit family, and a little bit future, and she knew this feeling was more powerful than any magic.	• Our protagonist slows down to look at each of the secondary characters. We slow down with her. • At the center of this story is the power that magic lends our character. She feels it again, but here at the end she feels it differently than she did throughout the book. • Now she is _tired and tormented_ (alliteration). • When she feels the magic again, leaving her body, she realizes it is not what gives her power— a classic move in an ending. The character experiences the same sensation from early in the book in a new way. • This scene begins with a toast to friends and ends with the image of the three friends running together hand in hand. They are running away from us—the readers. Watching something leave is another way that endings feel right to us. • Thor uses the power of three to explain the flutter in Ingrid's veins. • The last phrase indicates that friendship is more powerful than magic, which is the moral of this story.

SECOND: IMITATE

The best way to practice endings is to first remember seminal moments in our lives. I have students consider events in a year or a place they have visited many times. Students who have lost pets often choose that as a subject. Others write of the end of playing a team sport or leaving middle school for high school. Many students have moved across town or to different states. We talk about how losing things can be sad, but some endings move us toward something we anticipate with joy or adventure or curiosity. We leave behind age 15, but now we can learn how to drive. We leave behind our childhood home, but we find two best friends in our new school.

I make a list of a few of my own life transitions and encourage students to do the same in their notebooks:

- Moving upstairs with my class from our fifth-grade classroom for grades six to eight.

- The last time I walked to my elementary school.

- Moving from our house on Belmont Street to a town and school four hours south.

- Selling my three-speed bike to a younger kid in the neighborhood and coming home to ride my 10-speed bike down the big hill with no hands. Feeling so much older.

When I have several ideas, I show students how I "try on" each one as a possible topic by saying, "I can remember feeling like I was grown up when I walked those stairs to the upper level of my K–8 school. I think about the stairwell and so much of that time comes back to me. I like this topic....

Although I can imagine that last walk to the school, I don't think I have as much to say about it.

The third idea—moving away—was important in our family, but I was only in first grade, so I don't remember much.

The bike idea is a good one. I'm going to hang on to that. I think I have a lot to say about riding no hands. But, today, I'm going to try to write about the first one on my list."

It is important to show students how writers might hold on to topics for future projects. We are all full of many ideas for writing. I give students a few moments to try on their own topics and select one to work with that day. I ask students to talk through their ideas with a partner, while I walk the room listening in. I take my notebook and list comments that I can use in my lesson to benefit all students:

> "I remember this moment so well! I can see all the details..."
> "That was the time when I knew I was done with soccer. I could write about that."

When I bring students together, I share student comments and reinforce what we have learned so far. I say, "It is wise to choose a subject where you remember a lot of details. We know that readers want sensory details to engage fully in the experience you are writing about." Sharing students' comments often spurs ideas. After all, the ideas of classmates are usually more inspiring than their teacher's ideas.

I invite students to begin writing as I do. "I want to imitate the moves the author makes in *Fire Becomes Her*. One move is the way she looks back at her friends that have been with her throughout the story." I write:

> I make a quick right turn when I reach the stairs and put my foot on the first one. Beside me are my two best friends, Julia and Cynthia. Both have worn their hair today brushed out in long waves, not braided like we all wore our hair in fifth grade. We admire our new shoes, knocking the toes together step by step. I take a breath and look up to the large window which frames the landing above. The sun is bright this morning: my first day of sixth grade. Students race by us. I want to hold on to the moment just like I hold on to the railing with my left hand. This is what it means to grow up, I think.

I tell students, "I'm going to make a list of moments from elementary school that I might have remembered as I walked up the stairs." I name the craft move "the list" to remind students of the tools they have learned that are always available to them.

> I remember nap time in kindergarten: our rugs arranged in parallel lines across the floor, the lights low, the hum of the heater, and the

snores of Julia and Cynthia lying beside me. I remember choosing picture books in the library before I could read all the words. I remember running to the playground for recess holding hands with Julia on one side and Cynthia on the other. I remember hiding in the custodian's closet after school when my mom had to go in and talk to my third grade teacher. I knew I was in trouble, and I didn't want to face it. I heard Julia and Cynthia calling for me.

Remember, students might still be listing ideas as you begin your draft, and that's okay. Being in a room of fellow writers, thinking and working in notebooks together, is important. We are all figuring things out as writers, even if we are at different points in our writing. I go back and silently reread what I've written above and add more:

All those memories reminded me of how much we had learned in our six years in the lower grades. What was ahead for us in sixth, seventh, and eighth grades? My stomach fluttered and rolled, but my eyes focused straight ahead as I turned the corner for the last flight of stairs. I could do this. Instead of addition there would be Algebra, instead of recess games I would be trying out for the basketball team, and instead of walking home with Julia and Cynthia each afternoon I planned to walk with Russell Zavodsky. I couldn't wait to begin.[93]

In this demonstration, I have captured the feel of an ending, but there is an important move I have yet to try. I want to capture an important lesson learned in fifth grade that I carry into sixth grade. I tell students I have to think more about that before I am ready to write it.

As with most first drafts, as I reread this one now, I see places I want to revise. There are words and phrases I can fiddle with to make better. I might expand the list of memories to include art class or the school play in fifth grade. I might mention teachers I liked or even the way my friends and I noticed the older kids on the playground and wondered what it was like to be in middle school. And then, in the end, what did I learn? I'm not sure, but the more I write, the more likely it is to come to me. So many possibilities. So many things to write.

---

[93] I bet you noticed the power of three *and* intentional repetition in this paragraph. Isn't it fun to recognize the moves you make as you practice them with students? They become ingrained in us, just as they will in our students.

The three endings below show various craft moves at work. Choose one you feel is a good fit for your students and use it to deepen an understanding of combining craft moves, as I did in the last section.

Lines of Courage by Jennifer A. Nielsen

The Lasting Impact of World War I

By the end of the war, almost forty million people, including civilians and soldiers, had lost their lives, and millions more were wounded, displaced from their homes and villages. The war would redraw world maps, topple empires, and change the trajectory of world history.

Most historians will say that as destructive as World War I was, the real tragedy is that it led to nearly a century of conflict throughout the world.

Certainly there were many reasons why World War I began, but it is a curious thing to wonder how history might have been different, if only a driver in Bosnia had not taken a wrong turn one afternoon in June.

With the Might of Angels by Andrea Davis Pinkney

Wednesday, May 18, 1955

Diary Book,

Happy Birthday to Me! I haven't written in a while for the simple reason that this book's pages have run low because of Goober's scribbling, and I wanted to save some space for writing on my birthday.

As it turns out, I now have enough pages to write for at least another year. I'm in bed as I fill up on writing. My red pencil is short now, but its point is still as sharp as ever.

This morning the in-between had nothing on me. I was awake while the moon started to wave good-bye. The sky was peeling open to let in the sun.

Something hard-edged poked through my pillow's softness, I knew right off what it was, and reached around to pull it out from its hiding place.

It's a new Diary Book![94] For my thirteenth birthday! From Goober!

I will never use the bad *H* word about my brother again. He has given me a new *H* word to describe how I feel about him. I am *humbled* by how good a soul that boy is.

My new diary has a green fabric cover and a pocket in the back. I can tell by the lavender smell coming off the book's front and by the stiff-stiff way it's been sewn together that Mama's had a hand in making it. The book has been pressed with an iron, I just know it.

The pages are the same as this diary's pages, rough at the edges from the way Goober's cut them to fit between the new book's covers. Goober's written a note on the book's inside front: I recognize his handwriting. It says:

To Dawnie. My sister. You can fly.

Now I have reached this book's last page. It's just as well. I need to stop writing. Goober's calling me.

"Dawnie, come out and play!"

The Sky Is Everywhere by Jandy Nelson

I reach for my pack, pull a small notebook out of it. I transcribed all the letters Gram wrote to our mom over the last sixteen years. I want Bailey to have those words. I want her to know that there will never be a story that she won't be a part of, that she's everywhere like the sky[95]. I open the door and slide the book in the little cabinet, and as I do, I hear something scrape. I reach in and pull out a ring. My stomach drops. It's gorgeous, an orange topaz, big as an acorn. Perfect for Bailey. Toby must have had it made especially for her. I hold it in my palm and the certainty that she never got to see it pierces me. I bet the ring is what they were waiting for to finally tell us about their marriage, the baby. How Bails would've showed it off when they made the grand announcements. I rest it on the edge of the stone where it catches a glint of the sun and throws amber prismatic light over all the engraved words.

---

[94] I always hope, at the start of each school year, that students will find the gift of a writer's notebook exciting. When we value notebooks, when we value the craft moves our students make in them, and when we value their individual voices, excitement happens.

[95] I just love it when a novel ends with the words of the title. Suddenly I understand how it all fits together.

I try to fend off the oceanic sadness, but I can't. It's such a colossal effort not to be haunted by what's lost, but to be enchanted by what was.

I miss you, I tell her, *I can't stand that you're going to miss so much.*

I don't know how the heart withstands it.

I kiss the ring, put it back into the cabinet next to the notebook, and close the door with the bird on it. Then I reach into my pack and take out the houseplant. It's so decrepit, just a few blackened leaves left. I walk over to the edge of the cliff, so I'm right over the falls. I take the plant out of its pot, shake the dirt off the roots, get a good drip, reach my arm back, take one deep breath before I pitch my arm forward, and let go.

Their Turn: Independent Practice

Beginnings and endings are powerful markers in literature. Perhaps you've memorized the opening lines of your favorite novels, as I have. Perhaps you've sat on your couch with a book in hand, surprised to see you have reached the last page, and intentionally slowed your reading to make that moment last.

Remember: There is an important difference between reading to understand what is happening and reading to understand why an author crafted the text in a particular way. When you study *how* a passage or chapter is crafted, you are inviting students into rhetorical reading. I watched an expert teacher leading a pre-AP ninth-grade class this week, and as the students struggled, I was struck by how sophisticated it is to read with the author's craft in mind. *Micro Mentor Texts* is designed to break this skill into parts that students learn over time. It prepares them for all the reading and writing they will do in the future.

Conclusion

Endings have power. It's probably why I've struggled to write this one. One of my favorite craft moves for bringing a piece to a close is called a circular ending or an echo, where the writer brings you back to where you started. It might be the cello music in the opening scene of the novel *If I Stay* by Gayle Forman. As the character rises from her body to survey the aftermath of a horrific crash, she says, "Then it went quiet, except for this: Beethoven's Cello Sonata no. 3, still playing. The car radio somehow still attached to a battery and so Beethoven is broadcasting into the once-again tranquil February morning."

At the end, her boyfriend puts headphones around her ears. The cello music plays, and you remember the journey the novel has taken you on. You imagine music might wake her, might bring her back from the coma she has been in since the accident. There is power in that echo.

I began this book by explaining how writing instruction in most schools has moved from freedom and creativity to test prep. Today, students write more formulaic essays than exploratory ones. They write little fiction, but lots of answers to questions in neat and orderly paragraphs. This shift was fueled by fear, not by what is best for young children. Teachers were handed curriculum and told to teach it—not with joy, not with passion, but rather, fidelity. Follow the rules.

There is so much more to explore in writing than rules. Great writer's craft is everywhere—and it often surprises us in the simplest forms, such as in a commercial or on a hotel sign. One afternoon, it grabbed me while standing by the cash register at Imelda's Shoes in Portland, Oregon.

OUR RETURN POLICY
(the Novel)

Being a small, plucky place our story begins on a sheepish

sorry, no refunds note, but lightens up considerably with an offer of

store credit or exchange within 7 days of purchase.

The stylish have the unalienable right to reconsider, after all.

Then the small print arrives. Ironically, in quite bold letters.

All merchandise must be returned in its original package.

Future shoppers, studies show, frown on new pumps in old 7–11 sacks.

Then the plot thickens: **shoes must not show wear.**

Lest unscrupulous buyers use the one-date-and-return trick.

And, as much as we'd like to, **we cannot guarantee the comfort of a shoe.**

So, take your fitting seriously. Unlike wedding vows.

Finally, **all sale merchandise is final.** But that's immaterial.
You look fantastic!

Like Audrey Hepburn and Gregory Peck in *Roman Holiday*.

THE END

I laughed and started reading it again, line by line. More than clever, this piece of writing is intentional and clear. It delivers information with zing and flair. I want to know (and mimic) this writer. So please indulge me in one last imitation:

OUR RETURN
(a Pledge)

Being spunky, unstoppable teachers, we promise

responsive, student-centered practices, strengthened considerably

by decades of research on reading, writing,

and the expansive powers of both.

Professional teachers, after all, have labored to understand

the needs of individual young people and we know that

courage, thoughtfulness, and laughter in teaching

hold more power than mandates.

We are leery of standardized curriculum, cellophane-wrapped

promises of standards! Test prep! Proficiency!

Because the small print arrives ironically in big, bold letters:

We hired you for passion and vision, but we don't actually

trust you to make decisions about teaching.

The plot thickens: the standards and strategies multiply yearly

while many—far too many—young readers and writers are miserable.

There is an answer.

Take your agency seriously. Unlike dress codes.

Remember you know your students better than anyone.

You lead with vision and voice,

and **your model of playfulness and joy in writing is contagious.**

Like Mandy Patinkin and Robin Wright in *The Princess Bride*.

This work will change your teaching.

And writing your life

will change **you.**

THE END

Acknowledgments

For the team at Scholastic who have helped me bring this book to you: Tara Welty, Sarah Longhi, Shelley Griffin, Danny Miller, and Samantha Unger, my gratitude stretches shore to shore, like the last bit of light before dark. To the designers, Tannaz Fassihi and Maria Lilja, you brought beauty to every page. I see your attention to color and space. You leave breathing room for readers. Thank you.

For my editor Ray Coutu, your kindness and keen attention to each line carried me to this final draft. You are a terrific reader and a gentle, but insistent craftsman. Every time I lost the throughline in a chapter, you noticed. Every time I stumbled, you asked questions. And for Lois Bridges, who helped me imagine this book, I am sorry for the multi-year delay. Here, finally, is the book we dreamed up together. Your heart for children is knit closely to mine. Thank you always for your vision.

To 39 years of students, it is your imitations and expansions of lines we read in class that continue to ignite me with joy. Your courage to write is in these pages. Thanks also to the staff and volunteers at Emma L. Andrews Library and Community Center in Newburyport, Massachusetts, and the families that participated in the photo shoot.

To my family: Cam, Hannah, Ellen, Maisie, Lila, and Pat, you read me better than anyone. You write beauty into the every day. I love you all more than coffee, more than the sunrise across the water, more than my writing notebooks. I am so blessed to live my life beside you.

References

Alexander, Kwame. "List Poetry and the Art of Classroom Storytelling." Scholastic EDU, Nov. 24, 2015.

Allington, Richard L. "What I've Learned About Effective Reading Instruction From a Decade of Studying Exemplary Elementary Classroom Teachers." *The Phi Delta Kappan*, June 2002.

Atwell, Nancie. 2017. *Lessons that Change Writers*. Heinemann.

Atwell, Nancie. 2014. *In the Middle: New Understandings About Writing, Reading, and Learning, Third Edition*. Heinemann.

Beers, Kylene, & Robert E. Probst, presentation at the Boothbay Literacy Retreat, Edgecomb, ME. June 26, 2013.

Bridges, Lois. 2007. "RTI: The Best Intervention Is a Good Book." Scholastic.

Bridges, Lois, ed. 2014. *Open a World of Possible: Real Stories About the Joy and Power of Reading*. Scholastic.

Elbow, Peter, & Pat Belanoff. 1999. *Sharing and Responding, Third Edition*. McGraw-Hill.

Essley, Roger, Linda Rief & Amy Levy Rocci. 2008. *Visual Tools for Differentiating Reading & Writing Instruction*. Scholastic.

Graves, Donald H. 1978. *Balance the Basics: Let Them Write*. Ford Foundation, New York.

Graves, Donald H. 1980. *Writing: Teachers and Children at Work*. Heinemann.

Kittle, Penny. 2021. *Book Love: Developing Depth, Stamina, and Passion in Adolescent Readers*. Heinemann.

Lane, Barry. "Explode a Moment," posted to YouTube, Feb. 8, 2011.

Miller, Donalyn. "The 2021 Nerdies: Poetry and Novels in Verse." Nerdy Book Club, Dec. 30, 2021.

Murray, Donald M. 1991. As quoted in Rief, Linda. Heinemann.

Murray, Donald M. 2007. University of Southern New Hampshire Writing Conference.

Newkirk, Thomas. 2021. *Writing Unbound*. Heinemann.

Newkirk, Tom, & Penny Kittle. 2013. *Children Want to Write: Don Graves and the Revolution in Children's Writing*. Heinemann.

Reynolds, Jason. 2017. "How Poetry Can Help Kids Turn a Fear of Literature Into Love." PBS News Hour, Dec. 15, 2017.

Rief, Linda. 2018. *The Quickwrite Handbook: 100 Mentor Texts to Jumpstart Your Students' Thinking and Writing*. Heinemann.

Romano, Tom. 2000. *Blending Genre, Altering Style*. Heinemann.

Sims Bishop, Rudine. Video interview, Jan. 30, 2015, https://www.readingrockets.org/teaching/experts/rudine-sims-bishop

U.S. Department of Education, National Commission on Excellence in Education, 1983. *A Nation at Risk: The Imperative for Education Reform*. University of Michigan Library.

Writing Next, Carnegie Corporation, 2007.

LITERATURE AND OTHER SOURCES CITED

Abdel-Fattah, Randa. *The Lines We Cross*. Scholastic, 2018.

Alexander, K. R. *Vacancy*. Scholastic, 2021.

Bascomb, Neal. *The Race of the Century: The Battle to Break the Four-Minute Mile*. Scholastic, 2022.

Betts, A. J. *Zac & Mia*. Houghton Mifflin Harcourt, 2016.

Big 7 Travel, "The 50 Best Places for Chicken Wings in the USA." Nov. 11, 2020.

Booth, Coe. *Caprice*, Scholastic, 2022.

Booth, Coe. *Tyrell*, PUSH, 2007.

Callender, Kacen. *King and the Dragonflies*, Scholastic (US), 2020.

Callender, Kacen. *Hurricane Child*, Scholastic, 2018.

Cameron, Sharon. *The Light in Hidden Places*, Scholastic, 2021.

Cervantes, Angela. *Me, Frida, and the Secret of the Peacock Ring*, Scholastic, 2019.

Cleary, Beverly. *The Mouse and the Motorcycle*, HarperCollins, 1965.

Cullen, Countee. "Incident," *My Soul's High Song: The Collected Writings of Countee Cullen*, Anchor Books, 1991.

de la Peña, Matt. *Infinity Ring: Curse of the Ancients*, Scholastic, 2013.

de la Peña, Matt. *The Living*, Ember, 2015.

de la Peña, Matt. Personal interview, March 17, 2017, Bangkok.

Fitzhugh, Louise. *Harriet the Spy*, Harper & Row, 1964.

Forman, Gayle. *If I Stay*, Speak, 2009.

Fox, Helena. *How It Feels to Float*, Dial Books, 2019.

Freeman, Megan. *Alone*, Aladdin, 2021.

Gansworth, Eric. *If I Ever Get Out of Here*, Arthur A. Levine Books, 2015.

Gino, Alex. *Rick*. Scholastic, 2020.

Gino, Alex. *Alice Austen Lived Here*, Scholastic, 2022.

Gratz, Alan. *Refugee*. Scholastic, 2017.

Green, John. *The Anthropocene Reviewed: Essays on a Human-Centered Planet*, Dutton, 2021.

Heard, Georgia. *Falling Down the Page*, Square Fish, 2009.

Johnson, Varian. *The Great Greene Heist*, Arthur E. Levine Books, 2015.

Lewis, C. S. *The Chronicles of Narnia*, Macmillan, 1970.

Myers, Walter Dean. *Sunrise Over Fallujah*, Scholastic, 2009.

Myers, Walter Dean. *Somewhere in the Darkness*, Scholastic, 2008.

Nelson, Jandy. *The Sky Is Everywhere*, Penguin, 2011.

Nielsen, Jennifer A. *Lines of Courage*, Scholastic, 2022.

Older, Daniel José. *Shadowshaper*. Scholastic, 2016.

Owens, Delia. *Where the Crawdads Sing*. Penguin, 2021.

Pilkey, Dav. *The Paperboy*, Orchard Books, 2016

Pinkney, Andrea Davis. *Rhythm Ride*, Roaring Brook Press, 2016.

Pinkney, Andrea Davis. *With the Might of Angels*, Scholastic, 2019.

Pinkney, Andrea Davis. *Martin Rising: Requiem for a King*, Scholastic, 2018.

Pinkney, Andrea Davis. *Boycott Blues: How Rosa Parks Inspired a Nation*, Greenwillow Books, 2021.

Pinkney, Andrea Davis. *The Red Pencil*, Little, Brown Books, 2015.

Pinkney, Andrea Davis. *Duke Ellington: The Piano Prince and His Orchestra*, Hyperion, 2007.

Reynolds, Jason. *Long Way Down*, Atheneum/Caitlyn Dlouhy Books, 2019.

Reynolds, Justin A. *It's the End of the World and I'm in My Bathing Suit*, Scholastic, 2022.

Roche, Patrick. "21," *Button Poetry* on YouTube, 2014.

Rosenthal, Amy Krause. "You May Want to Marry My Husband," *The New York Times*, March 3, 2017.

Rowling, J. K. *Harry Potter and the Sorcerer's Stone*, Scholastic, 1998.

Ryan, Pam Muñoz. *Amelia and Eleanor Go for a Ride*, Scholastic, 1999.

Ryan, Pam Muñoz. *Paint the Wind*, Scholastic, 2009.

Ryan, Pam Muñoz. *The Dreamer*, Scholastic, 2010.

Ryan, Pam Muñoz. *When Marian Sang: The True Recital of Marian Anderson*, Scholastic, 2002.

Rylant, Cynthia. *The Great Gracie Chase: Stop That Dog!* Scholastic, 2001

Salazar, Aida. *Land of the Cranes*, Scholastic, 2020.

Salazar, Aida. *The Moon Within*, Arthur A. Levine Books, 2019.

Sitomer, Alan Lawrence. *Caged Warrior*, Scholastic. 2015.

Soontornvat, Christina. *A Wish in the Dark*, Candlewick, 2020.

Steele, Amanda. "Game of Thrones: 10 Things Fans Are Most Upset About From the Series Finale," *Screenrant*, May 23, 2019.

Steinbeck, John. *Of Mice and Men*, Penguin, 1993.

Stork, Francisco X. *Illegal*, Scholastic, 2020.

Teague, Mark. *Dear Mrs. LaRue: Letters from Obedience School*, Scholastic, 2007.

Thor, Rosiee. *Fire Becomes Her*, Scholastic, 2022.

Touropia. "10 Best Museums in Rome," Sep. 7, 2020.

Wang, Andrea. *Watercress*, Neal Porter Books, 2021.

Wiles, Deborah. *Countdown*, Scholastic, 2016.

Willingham, AJ. "What Would Make You Care About Aleppo?" CNN. April 4, 2016.

Index

A
Abdel-Fattah, Randa, 56, 94, 157–158
"academic" voice, 111
achievement, assessments of, 10
acronyms, 90
actions, describing, 50–58, 72–74
adjective-noun pattern, 43, 63, 70
Alexander, K. R., 106, 154–157
Alice Austen Lived Here (Alex Gino), 144–145, 147–148
alliteration, 35, 59, 66, 69, 113, 142, 143, 161
Alone, "Model Home" (Megan Freeman), 112–118
Amelia and Eleanor Go for a Ride (Pam Muñoz Ryan), setting revealed in, 18
anchor chart, use of, 21, 36–37
annotating thinking, students', 108
assessment, 138–139
assonance, 143
Atwell, Nancie, 12, 98, 129
audiobooks, 35

B
background information, providing, 101, 104–105
background knowledge, 30–31, 62
Bascomb, Neal, 58
beginnings, craft moves in, 154–159
best friend, as topic, 52–53
Betts, A. J., 43–45
big idea, vs. everyday moments, 41
Bishop, Rudine Sims, 29
Black, Lauren, 53
Blending Genre, Altering Style (Tom Romano), 121
book access, 23
book clubs, 45, 75–76, 138
Booth, Coe, 79, 84, 89, 91–93
Boycott Blues (Andrea Davis Pinkney), 69–70
"breathing space," 79
Bridges, Lois, 9, 31
Brontë, Charlotte, her first drafts, 59

C
Caged Warrior (Alan Sitomer), 23–26
Callendar, Kacen, 19–20, 27, 33, 41–42, 85–88, 119
Cameron, Sharon, 57
Caprice (Coe Booth), 84, 89, 91–93
Cervantes, Angela, 22, 28
characters
   capturing their conversations, 85–89
   dialogue to reveal, 79–85
   list to describe, 41–46
   sensory details to reveal, 23–30
chart paper, use of, 44
Chicagoland, 39
choosing a topic, modeled, 162–163
Chronicles of Narnia, The (C. S. Lewis), 23
cicadas, 43, 44, 101
claim, asserted, 43, 101
Cofer, Judith Ortiz, 140
collaborative writing, 95
competition among students, 20, 68
conferring, one-on-one, 13, 76
connection with reader, establishing, 24
consonance, 18, 114, 143
conventions, 121
Countdown (Deborah Wiles), 54
creation vs. imitation, 20
crossing out, modeled, 25–26
Cullen, Countee, 122
curriculum, standardization of, 13

D
de la Peña, Matt, 49, 71, 88
Dear Mrs. LaRue: Letters from Obedience School (Mark Teague), 128
decision-making, modeled, 73–74, 82–83
details, 17–18, 62–65, 134
   defining actions with three, 72–74
   describing event with three, 65–68
   describing experience with three, 69–71
   precise, 62–65
   sensory, 16–37, 51, 52, 80, 99, 160
dialogue, 24, 77–95, 101
   attributions in, 85
   characters revealed by, 79–85
   in endings, 160
   paragraphing of, 106–107
   of text messages, 89–94

discovery, through writing process, 98–100, 111–117
double-speak, 78–79
drafts, first, 59–60
Dreamer, The (Pam Muñoz Ryan), 54, 146
Duke Ellington: The Piano Prince and His Orchestra (Andrea Davis Pinkney), 119

E
echoing, 42, 114, 115
educational reform, history of, 9–13
Elbow, Peter, 8, 116
emails, 90–91, 129–130
emotional cues, for writing, 87
endings, craft moves in, 153, 160–167
engagement in classroom, 106
Essley, Roger, 133
event, described with three details, 65–68
everyday moments, 41
experience, described with three details, 69–71
"Exploding a Moment," 97
extended metaphor, 86, 144, 160
extended writing, 13

F
Falling Down the Page: A Book of List Poems (Georgia Heard), 39
favorite things, lists of, 68
feelings, strong, as topic, 86–87
fiction, voice in, 112–119
fiction vs. nonfiction, 52–53, 155
Fire Becomes Her (Rosiee Thor), 136, 160–164
"First Chapter Fridays," 153
first lines, list of, 41
"fixin's for the soul," 63
"flash fiction," 155–157
flashbacks/flash-forwards, 132, 134
fonts, 121
fragments, 51, 69, 91, 92, 113
Freeman, Megan, 112–118
freewriting, 68, 116

G
Gansworth, Eric, 55
genre, choice of, 121